Peace Is Possible

FRANZ ALT

PEACE IS POSSIBLE

The Politics of the Sermon on the Mount

TRANSLATED FROM THE GERMAN
BY JOACHIM NEUGROSCHEL

SCHOCKEN BOOKS · NEW YORK

First published by Schocken Books 1985
10 9 8 7 6 5 4 3 2 1   85 86 87 88
English translation copyright © 1985 by Schocken Books Inc.
Originally published in German as Frieden ist möglich:
Die Politik der Bergpredigt by R. Piper & Co. Verlag;
copyright © R. Piper & Co. Verlag, Munich 1983

Library of Congress Cataloging in Publication Data
Alt, Franz.
    Peace is possible.
    Translation of: Frieden ist möglich.
    1. Sermon on the mount. 2. Christianity and
politics. 3. Peace—Religious aspects—Christianity.
I. Title.
BT380.2.A6713   1985   261.7   84-23499

    Designed by Jacqueline Schuman
    Manufactured in the United States of America
    ISBN 0-8052-3969-3

We gratefully acknowledge the National Council of the
Churches of Christ for permission to reprint the Sermon on the
Mount from the Revised Standard Version of the Bible,
copyrighted 1946, 1952 © 1971, 1973.

for Christiane and Caren Maria

CONTENTS

ONE

The Sermon on the Mount

Blessed are the peacemakers.
—Jesus

The Sermon on the Mount Is Not a Regional Novel

Is peace possible? What does the Sermon on the Mount say? The Sermon on the Mount tells us what Christians should be like—if they are Christians. My interest in the Sermon is personal and fundamental, not academic. Nothing is more powerful than the idea whose time has come. I feel that our time is ripe for the idea of the Sermon on the Mount. In times of the greatest violence, people must look to nonviolence.

I realize that many readers agree with my political thoughts but reject my religious arguments against nuclear arms. Many people do not need the arguments of the Sermon on the Mount: they reject nuclear weapons on purely humanistic grounds. Others may go along with my religious interpretation of the Sermon, but they regard the political consequences as dangerous. West German Chancellor Helmut Kohl wrote me as much in a letter.

However, during the past few years, I have come to see humanism, religion, politics, and mental development as inextricable. They are not identical, but they belong together. Our religious, private, and political existence is one. Being human means being an individual in the original sense of the word: indivisible. The worst schism in Christendom was not Martin Luther's rupture of the church. It was the separation of religion and politics. This modern schism cuts a human being into religious *or* political, pious *or* intelligent, theological *or* philosophical, spiritual *or* technological; into Christian feelings *or* materialistic actions. The ultimate consequence of this split is a liturgical Sunday church on one side and a secular workday on the other.

In the industrial countries, Christianity has deteriorated into a spineless middle-class ideology. Christianity as a massage of the soul, but with no repentance, no change of heart—religion as private business.

This Christianity, in a very un-Christian way, is scared of taking sides, of commitment. It is afraid of making waves and stirring up a fuss. If Christian charity can be experienced only privately, then it will not be experienced very long. For a while, we may be able to separate religion from politics and politics from private and professional life. But no one can lead a schizo-phrenic life forever. Today, the popular political split between an ethics of conviction and an ethics of responsibility is a schizo-phrenia with fearful consequences. This separation is a schism. As a result, many politicians feel themselves to be Christian in their private lives but do not know how to bring Jesus of Naza-reth into politics. Their faith in him is sentimental; politically, they consider him a fool. He's good for Sunday sermons and Christmas speeches. But in everyday political life, we are told, they don't have much use for him. That's why many politicians pay lip service to the master of nonviolence and simultaneously prepare the way for the atomic holocaust. Yet Jesus' nonvio-lence, like Gandhi's *ahimsa,* is active, not passive.

More than anything else, the books of C. G. Jung have helped me find a new approach to Jesus of Nazareth and to his central statements in the Sermon on the Mount. This is what made me a pacifist in regard to nuclear arms. My resistance to the increasingly complicated and increasingly dangerous "bal-ance of terror" comes from inside me—after a long meditation on the Sermon and our present-day situation. My source is Jesus of Nazareth, and Jung's psychological ideas have given me a new approach to my source.

In 1981, I believed that NATO had to keep up the arms race. Today, I consider it lethal. The reasons for my change of

heart are described in this book. It will take you about four hours
to read it. During these four hours, the world will spend something like a quarter of a billion dollars on arms. At the same
time, 7,000 children will starve to death. If things go on as in the
past twenty years, these figures will double by the year 2000.
Today, a child starves to death every two seconds. This is an
unendurable sin, and no one who claims to be a human being or
to believe in Jesus can put up with it.

For many people, Jesus of Nazareth is the hero of an ancient
story. But once you deal with him totally—that is, privately,
socially, professionally, and politically—you realize that the crucial question of your life is not "Who *was* Jesus?" but "Who *is*
Jesus?" To gain this insight, one needs an overwhelming experience, a Damascus experience.

In 1978, I wrote an article for the German newsmagazine *Der
Spiegel*, discussing the political platform of West Germany's
Christian Democratic party. The title of my article was "The
Sermon on the Mount Is Not a Regional Novel." This was the
straw that broke the camel's back for me. The Sermon took hold
of me and has been haunting me ever since. Sometimes I feel as
if it had been waiting for me for a long time. I am not a theologian. As a political journalist, I am a nontheologian with theological interests. You don't have to be a theologian to grasp the
meaning and the spirit of the Sermon on the Mount. And that's
all that counts. Not theological hair-splitting. Jesus didn't care
how many angels could dance on the head of a pin.

Today, even atheists cite the teacher of nonviolence. Liberals consider his Sermon on the Mount liberal, revolutionaries
find it revolutionary, and conservatives conservative. I am a
conservative who regards the Sermon above all as a human docu-
ment. Jesus does not speak to us in shallow terms. He addresses
our very core, intimately and wholeheartedly. As far as Jesus is
concerned, the private and the political cannot be kept apart.

The separation of the private and the political has always spelled doom for Christianity. Jesus spoke not only to theologians, but to the people. And *all* people are meant, in *all* walks of life. No Christian can sidestep the Sermon on the Mount. It contains the essence of Christianity. If you meditate on it intensively enough, you won't need anyone to interpret it for you. You have to take the words as they are written; you have to take Jesus at his word! Then, gradually (not all at once), things that were obscure will become clear. The Sermon is a road to knowledge of yourself and knowledge of the world.

Today, the world is an atomic powder keg. Several tons of explosives are prepared for every single human being. The world has more explosives per capita than food. The outcome can be deadly. However, each danger offers an opportunity to escape it. Because of the worldwide nuclear threat, we have a far greater chance of understanding the peace tidings of the Sermon than did earlier generations.

Its teachings are relevant not just in a superficial sense. With the atomic holocaust looming ahead of us, I am convinced that there is only one alternative to the Sermon on the Mount: the end of human history. The Austrian philosopher Günther Anders has summed it up aptly: "Either we will have peacetime or we will have no time. Peacetime and time per se have become identical."

Either we will learn to love our enemies and abolish nuclear bombs, or the nuclear bombs will abolish us. Heinrich Himmler wanted to make Europe free of Jews; atomic bombs can someday make the world free of human beings. In our situation, the preacher on the mount tells us: "Peace is possible. You only have to really want it." Jesus promises us something possible, not something unattainable.

By opposing the arms race today rather than defending it as I did in 1981, I am also admitting that I am still searching. I have written this book for the seekers and the doubters—for those who ask questions and want to know whether everything can go on as before. This book is for those who wish to know where the arms race is taking us. I do not wish to be right while others are wrong. I want to work with other people toward finding a better road to peace. Or is there really no humane alternative to the armaments madness?

The Western slogan is "Better dead than red." And I consider this as inhumane as the Communist watchword: "Better dead than capitalist." Many politicians are beginning to sense, albeit dimly, that the nonstop arms race no longer offers any security. Helmut Kohl said in October 1982 that the task of our time is "to create peace with fewer and fewer weapons." And, since mid-1982 East German Chancellor Erich Honecker has repeatedly said, "More weapons do not mean more security."

These two top-ranking German politicians now ought to make their actions speak louder than words. As Jesus said, we shall know them not by their words but "by their fruits."

People are once again arguing about the Sermon on the Mount. It is finally where it belongs: in public. Newspapers are printing the text. And some Christians, who may have a Bible at home but do not know where the Sermon is, have torn out the newspaper reprint in order to have the biblical text at least in this form.

The Sermon on the Mount (Matthew 5–7)

Seeing the crowds, [Jesus] went up on the mountain, and when he sat down his disciples came to him. And he opened his mouth and taught them, saying:

Blessed are the poor in spirit, for theirs is the kingdom of heaven.

Blessed are those who mourn, for they shall be comforted.

Blessed are the meek, for they shall inherit the earth.

Blessed are those who hunger and thirst for righteousness, for they shall be satisfied.

Blessed are the merciful, for they shall obtain mercy.

Blessed are the pure in heart, for they shall see God.

Blessed are the peacemakers, for they shall be called sons of God.

Blessed are those who are persecuted for righteousness' sake, for theirs is the kingdom of heaven.

Blessed are you when men revile you and persecute you and utter all kinds of evil against you falsely on my account. Rejoice and be glad, for your reward is great in heaven, for so men persecuted the prophets who were before you.

You are the salt of the earth; but if salt has lost its taste, how shall its saltness be restored? It is no longer good for anything except to be thrown out and trodden under foot by men.

You are the light of the world. A city set on a hill cannot be hid. Nor do men light a lamp and put it under a bushel, but on a stand, and it gives light to all in the house. Let your light so shine before men, that they may see your good works and give glory to your Father who is in heaven.

Think not that I have come to abolish the law and the prophets; I have come not to abolish them but to fulfil them. For truly, I say to you, till heaven and earth pass away, not an iota, not a dot, will pass from the law until all is accomplished. Whoever then relaxes one of the least of these commandments and teaches men so, shall be called least in the kingdom of heaven; but he who does them and teaches them shall be called great in the kingdom of heaven. For I tell you, unless your righteousness exceeds that of the scribes and Pharisees, you will never enter the kingdom of heaven.

You have heard that it was said to the men of old, "You shall not kill; and whoever kills shall be liable to judgment." But I say to you that every one who is angry with his brother shall be liable to judgment; whoever insults his brother shall be liable to the council, and whoever says, "You fool!" shall be liable to the hell of fire. So if you are offering your gift to the altar, and there remember that your brother has something against you, leave your gift there before the altar and go; first be reconciled to your brother, and then come and offer your gift. Make friends quickly with your accuser, while you are going with him to court, lest your accuser hand you over to the judge, and the judge to the guard, and you be put in prison; truly, I say to you, you will never get out till you have paid the last penny.

You have heard that it was said, "You shall not commit adultery." But I say to you that every one who looks at a woman lustfully has already committed adultery with her in his heart. If your right eye causes you to sin, pluck it out and throw it away; it is better that you lose one of your members than that your whole body be thrown into hell. And if your right hand causes you to sin, cut it off and throw it away; it is better that you lose one of your members than that your whole body go into hell.

It was also said, "Whoever divorces his wife, let him give her a certificate of divorce." But I say to you that every one who divorces his wife, except on the ground of unchastity, makes her an adulteress; and whoever marries a divorced woman commits adultery.

Again you have heard that it was said to the men of old, "You shall not swear falsely, but shall perform to the Lord what you have sworn." But I say to you, Do not swear at all, either by heaven, for it is the throne of God, or by the earth, for it is his footstool, or by Jerusalem, for it is the city of the great King. And do not swear by your head, for you cannot make one hair white or black. Let what you say be simply "Yes" or "No"; anything more than this comes from evil.

You have heard that it was said, "An eye for an eye and a

tooth for a tooth." But I say to you, Do not resist one who is evil. But if any one strikes you on the right cheek, turn to him the other also; and if any one would sue you and take your coat, let him have your cloak as well; and if any one forces you to go one mile, go with him two miles. Give to him who begs from you, and do not refuse him who would borrow from you.

You have heard that it was said, "You shall love your neighbor and hate your enemy." But I say to you, Love your enemies and pray for those who persecute you, so that you may be sons of your Father who is in heaven; for he makes his sun rise on the evil and on the good, and sends rain on the just and on the unjust. For if you love those who love you, what reward have you? Do not even the tax collectors do the same? And if you salute only your brethren, what more are you doing than others? Do not even the Gentiles do the same? You, therefore, must be perfect, as your heavenly Father is perfect.

Beware of practicing your piety before men in order to be seen by them; for then you will have no reward from your Father who is in heaven.

Thus, when you give alms, sound no trumpet before you, as the hypocrites do in the synagogues and in the streets, that they may be praised by men. Truly I say to you, they have their reward. But when you give alms, do not let your left hand know what your right hand is doing, so that your alms may be in secret; and your Father who sees in secret will reward you.

And when you pray, you must not be like the hypocrites; for they love to stand and pray in the synagogues and at the street corners, that they may be seen by men. Truly, I say to you, they have their reward. But when you pray, go into your room and shut the door and pray to your Father who is in secret; and your Father who sees in secret will reward you.

And in praying do not heap up empty phrases as the Gentiles do; for they think that they will be heard for their many words.

Do not be like them, for your Father knows what you need before you ask him. Pray then like this:

Our Father who art in heaven,
Hallowed be thy name.
Thy kingdom come,
Thy will be done,
On earth as it is in heaven.
Give us this day our daily bread;
And forgive us our debts,
As we also have forgiven our debtors;
And lead us not into temptation,
But deliver us from evil.

For if you forgive men their trespasses, your heavenly Father also will forgive you; but if you do not forgive men their trespasses, neither will your Father forgive your trespasses.

And when you fast, do not look dismal, like the hypocrites, for they disfigure their faces that their fasting may be seen by men. Truly, I say to you, they have their reward. But when you fast, anoint your head and wash your face, that your fasting may not be seen by men but by your Father who is in secret; and your Father who sees in secret will reward you.

Do not lay up for yourselves treasures on earth; where moth and rust consume and where thieves break in and steal, but lay up for yourselves treasures in heaven, where neither moth nor rust consumes and where thieves do not break in and steal. For where your treasure is, there will your heart be also.

The eye is the lamp of the body. So, if your eye is sound, your whole body will be full of light; but if your eye is not sound, your whole body will be full of darkness. If then the light in you is darkness, how great is the darkness!

No one can serve two masters; for either he will hate the one and love the other, or he will be devoted to the one and despise the other. You cannot serve God and mammon.

Therefore I tell you, do not be anxious about your life, what you shall eat or what you shall drink, nor about your body, what you shall put on. Is not life more than food, and the body more than clothing? Look at the birds of the air; they neither sow nor reap nor gather into barns, and yet your heavenly Father feeds them. Are you not of more value than they? And which of you by being anxious can add one cubit to his span of life? And why are you anxious about clothing? Consider the lilies of the field, how they grow; they neither toil nor spin; yet I tell you, even Solomon in all his glory was not arrayed like one of these. But if God so clothes the grass of the field, which today is alive and tomorrow is thrown into the oven, will he not much more clothe you, O men of little faith? Therefore do not be anxious, saying, "What shall we eat?" or "What shall we drink?" or "What shall we wear?" For the Gentiles seek all these things; and your heavenly Father knows that you need them all. But seek first his kingdom and his righteousness, and all these things shall be yours as well.

Therefore do not be anxious about tomorrow, but tomorrow will be anxious for itself. Let the day's own trouble be sufficient for the day.

Judge not, that you be not judged. For with the judgment you pronounce you will be judged, and the measure you give will be the measure you get. Why do you see the speck that is in your brother's eye, but do not notice the log that is in your own eye? Or how can you say to your brother, "Let me take the speck out of your eye," when there is the log in your own eye? You hypocrite, first take the log out of your own eye, and then you will see clearly to take the speck out of your brother's eye.

Do not give dogs what is holy; and do not throw your pearls before swine, lest they trample them underfoot and turn to attack you.

Ask, and it will be given you; seek and you will find; knock, and it will be opened to you. For every one who asks receives, and he who seeks finds, and to him who knocks it will be opened. Or what man of you, if his son asks him for a loaf, will give him a stone? Or if he asks for a fish, will give him a serpent? If you then, who are evil, know how to give good gifts to your children, how much more will your Father who is in heaven give good things to those who ask him? So whatever you wish that men would do to you, do so to them; for this is the law and the prophets.

Enter by the narrow gate; for the gate is wide and the way is easy, that leads to destruction, and those who enter by it are many. For the gate is narrow and the way is hard, that leads to life, and those who find it are few.

Beware of false prophets, who come to you in sheep's clothing but inwardly are ravenous wolves. You will know them by their fruits. Are grapes gathered from thorns, or figs from thistles? So, every sound tree bears good fruit, but the bad tree bears evil fruit. A sound tree cannot bear evil fruit, nor can a bad tree bear good fruit. Every tree that does not bear good fruit is cut down and thrown into the fire. Thus you will know them by their fruits.

Not every one who says to me, "Lord, Lord," shall enter the kingdom of heaven, but he who does the will of my Father who is in heaven. On that day many will say to me, "Lord, Lord, did we not prophesy in your name, and cast out demons in your name, and do many mighty works in your name?" And then will I declare to them, "I never knew you; depart from me, you evildoers."

Every one then who hears these words of mine and does them will be like a wise man who built his house upon the rock; and the rain fell, and the floods came, and the winds blew and beat upon that house, but it did not fall, because it had been founded on the rock. And every one who hears these words of mine and does not do them will be like a foolish man who built his house upon the sand; and the rain fell, and the floods came, and the winds blew and beat against that house, and it fell; and great was the fall of it.

And when Jesus finished these sayings, the crowds were astonished at his teaching, for he taught them as one who had authority, and not as their scribes.

Why the Sermon on the Mount Today?

Billions of copies of the Bible have been printed since Gutenberg. But no layman reads it through from start to finish. At best, you can read around in it. Even the church uses the Bible selectively in the course of the ecclesiastical year. Biblical passages are good for meditating, not for mechanical reading. The Sermon on the Mount is not the Bible; it is not even the New Testament. But it contains the essence of the tidings brought by Jesus. It exhales the spirit of Jesus like no other part of the Bible. In it, we find the central statements of the man from Nazareth.

The radical essence of Jesus, in its personal, social, and political consequences, is nowhere so obvious as in the Sermon on the Mount and the Sermon in the Fields (Luke 6). The Sermon on the Mount is not an authentic speech of Jesus', but it contains his authentic demands. It is a literary compilation of sayings by him. Its spirit is certainly his: nonviolence, peace, gentleness, caring for other people. The preacher on the mount is interested not so much in ascetic perfection as in human wholeness.

"You, therefore, must be perfect, as you heavenly Father is perfect." Everyone is addressed. At some point or other, we have to feel that peace and nonviolence are not just any policies. We have to realize that every single human being is meant, here and now. Only then can we begin to understand the Sermon on the Mount. Peace is not destiny. It is *our* mission, just as war is *our* failure. All of us occasionally make sublime ethical demands like those of the Sermon on the Mount; yet we regard them as impossible in our political and social reality.

The history of the Sermon on the Mount has not taken place. It is the story of the repression of its demands. Interestingly and understandably, people are still trying to mellow the intensity of the Sermon. Church leaders and theologians are still offering excuses for the hard line of the young Nazarene. Politicians say that Jesus is politically incompetent. Christians such as Otto von Bismarck, Helmut Schmidt, and Karl Carstens agree on one thing: "You can't govern with the Sermon on the Mount"—and no doubt there are American leaders who would agree. Hans Apel, as West German minister of defense, complained about the increase of pacifism (which Jesus demanded) and sneered, "In its totality, the Sermon on the Mount can be practiced only by mendicant monks." The Nazis always affixed the adjective "undignified" to their swearword "pacifist." And, in 1935, Archbishop Conrad Gröber of Freiburg wrote that the church "has rejected the excessive and feeble pacifism that views war as unlawful and un-Christian and allows injustice to rule freely."

The outcome of politics without the spirit of the Sermon on the Mount is obvious to anyone who has two eyes in his head. Economically, we live off future generations and off people in the so-called Third World. Militarily, we are preparing the end of creation. East and West together now have the possibility of destroying Hiroshima 1.6 million times! "Hiroshima is everywhere," said Günther Anders. And the arms race goes on. For every inhabitant of every country in NATO or the Warsaw Pact, there are sixty tons of explosives. The super death powers can kill one another at least twenty times. Yet this is far from adequate, according to Eastern and Western political leaders who keep up the arms race. No one seems capable of stopping. The atom bomb is not even forty years old and it is taken very seriously in politics. The Sermon on the Mount is two thousand years old, it is repeatedly quoted, and yet it plays no role in political practice. Even those who cite Jesus of Nazareth privately will shrug him off as a crackpot politically, a man who didn't know what he was talking about. His suggestion that we practice a policy of loving our enemies is regarded at best as charming political foolishness. This is the very reaction that Jesus prophesied. He was a realist.

Jesus was neither a priest nor a biblical scholar or theologian. He was a layman. It is not always easy to figure out what he really meant. He himself never wrote anything down. The four biblical biographers of Jesus, the Evangelists, did not know him personally (according to modern-day theology). They wouldn't even have understood his language. He spoke Aramaic. The language of the New Testament is Greek, the lingua franca of that period. And the Evangelists did not write until sixty years after Christ's birth. Their sources are difficult to reconstruct. Thus, the Evangelists do not present Jesus directly, but only a specific image of him. Some statements attributed to him in the Gospels not only do not come from Jesus, they actually contradict his spirit. The controversial literature on this subject fills libraries.

After several years of digging up the buried Jesus and removing the patina from the painted Jesus, I finally came upon the Jesus of the Sermon on the Mount. He is a prophet, not a philosopher. If you start to think about his statements in Matthew 5–7 and try to live in accordance with these words, you will realize that the God of Jesus is a God of love and peace.

Jesus turns right side up many things that were upside down. He cares about substance, not religious formulas. He cares about love, not formal justice; practice, not theory; peace actions, not peace chitchat; life, not doctrines.

Is the Sermon on the Mount applicable only for the paradisiacal end of days, or is it meant for this world? Contrary to what pious books say and what bombastic sermons state, the world of the Sermon is our world. Presumably, there will be no fighting and shooting in the next world, and no courts of law or prisons. The Sermon is about our world—from start to finish. Jesus' key words are "now" and "new."

His teachings are not meant as promises about some future life. He blesses the peacemakers. He offers us a better world. Once the Sermon on the Mount grabs hold of you, it fills you with Jesus' challenge: "I am the way, the truth, and the life." Nor does Jesus make any impossible demands, as has often been claimed. He is a brother, not a cruel despot playing an evil game with us. Jesus brought something radically new to the world. His ethics are not beyond the world; they are meant to change the world. He rejected any harmony with tradition and the status quo. "Neither is new wine put into old wineskins." (Matthew 9:17).

Ever since, the key question for his followers has been: Are you what you *can* be? Are you what you *should* be? Jesus demands no less than a revolution of our total consciousness, both private and political. Yet beyond any doubt, Christians and Christian churches, although about to enter the third Christian millennium, are still living as in pre-Christian days. Harmony with the state, the society, and private lifestyles are always more important to us than our Christian identity.

Today, we have at best the Christian consciousness of infants. We are afraid to become Christian adults. After the Enlightenment, the Western world became a scientific giant. But, spiritually and religiously, it remained a baby. And the fault, according to Hanna Wolff, lies with the still prevailing patriarchal conception of humanity and its sickening image of God.

The patriarchal consciousness involves "manly" values such as violence, obedience, achievement, commands, and reason. "Female" values (such as nonviolence, trust, love, and forgiveness) and feelings are as suppressed as they were two thousand years ago. Jesus is a man of feeling. Jesus' image of humanity—an integral image encompassing both male and female concepts—has had almost no effect on Christianity for two millennia. Not even his image of God as a loving father has been accepted. For Jesus, love means forgiving not seven times, but seventy times seven. Have we understood this yet? Yet even today we observe the primitive ethics of pagan times. In private, we always look for scapegoats, and politics is ruled by images of the enemy. Politicians who talk about peace are preparing for the annihilation of humanity.

The atomic "balance of terror" has no ethical basis in the Sermon on the Mount. The man who preached it was a challenge to his time. And he still is today. We have understood very little of what he said. His dialectic goes as follows: "You have heard that it was said to the men of old . . . But I say to you." I am no longer surprised that this provocateur wound up on the cross. I am only surprised that the rulers didn't bother him for three years.

"You are the salt of the earth. . . . You are the light of the world." Jesus wants to stir the imagination, so that it will picture a better world. He does not want a revolution for its own sake or reform for its own sake. Nor does he basically deny the religious and legal traditions of his people. He merely asks what they mean. Jesus always asks what something means. Religion, tradition, and politics have to exist for human beings, not vice versa. A human being is more important than the temple. Jesus wants human, voluntary, evolutionary progress, which challenges rather than begs the question posed by progress. Jesus prayed and went to the temple. He was patient with people. His patience was rooted in the knowledge that God lets His sun shine on both good and evil.

Is the Sermon on the Mount valid only for a chosen few?

Jesus addresses all people who are willing to listen. The Sermon is not just for his "disciples"; it is also for "the multitudes." "If you then, who are evil, know how to give good gifts to your children, how much more will your Father who is in heaven give good things to those who ask him?" It is comforting to know that the Sermon is meant also for those who are "evil."

The Sermon on the Mount contains private and political suggestions for living in the spirit of love. Prayer at home and marriage ethics are included, as well as love of one's enemy and an ethics of peace. And at the end, "the crowds were astonished at his teaching."

As a political journalist, I want to examine the consequences of the Sermon on the Mount for today's discussion of the politics of peace. A crucial insight to be gained from the Sermon is that only peaceful people can bring about political peace. The "false prophets" can be recognized by their deeds. "Thus you will know them by their fruits." That is, politicians who talk about peace but constantly prepare for war will never establish peace. "Every sound tree bears good fruit, but the bad tree bears evil fruit." Peace begins within us; the roots are decisive. Universal peace is contingent on individual efforts. Indeed, this applies to all realms of life.

Is the Sermon on the Mount Political?

Martin Luther distinguishes between personal and political ethics, between the "Christian person" and the "secular person": "A ruler can be a Christian, but he does not have to rule as a Christian, and by virtue of ruling, he is a ruler, not a Christian. The person is a Christian; but his office or rulership does not concern Christianity."

This is the double standard that most Christians still observe in politics. In theory, of course, one has to accept the Sermon on the Mount as an integral New Testament text. In practice, people look for excuses and ease their bad consciences by saying, "One can't govern with the Sermon on the Mount." And if this double standard is to sound intelligent and modern as well, then they quote Max Weber. Anything can be justified with his distinction between the ethics of conviction and the ethics of responsibility. A politician may advocate peace, but he considers it his responsibility to keep making nuclear bombs. Once, in a debate with me, a prominent German politician explained that, as a Christian, he certainly accepted the Sermon on the Mount, but, as a politician, he was responsible to both Christians and non-Christians, so the Sermon was not very useful. And since the Communists don't accept it, he said, there's no way that anyone can use it to pursue a politics of disarmament. The only thing that Communists understand, he concluded, is toughness.

Communists alone? Is the nuclear policy of the United States any less "tough"? Franz Josef Strauss advocates more and more armaments, yet claims to hold a "pacifist conviction." As a Christian, Strauss senses, of course, that you can't simply condemn pacifists if Jesus says that they are blessed. On the other hand, Strauss refuses to end the "balance of terror." Yet the Sermon on the Mount does not distinguish between freedom and responsibility. Radical freedom and radical responsibility are not antithetical. Radical freedom *is* radical responsibility.

The *ethics* of the Sermon on the Mount does not permit waffling. It demands an either/or. You cannot wish for the Sermon, you can only act upon it. The ethics of waffling is in the tradition of the Roman saying, "If you want peace, prepare for war!" Historically, such preparations have always led to war.

The *new ethics* of the Sermon, the ethics of either/or, demands the opposite: If you want peace, prepare for peace. If you prepare for war, you will get war. Good intentions are useless. Actions are what count. There is absolutely nothing in the Sermon about any division between private and political ethics. Jesus' justice is universal. The perfection he demands is linked to his criticism of the love that encompasses friends but not foes. According to him, love for your neighbor is not perfect unless it includes your enemies. This is political dynamite—which, to be sure, has almost never been practiced in the history of the world. Gandhi was the great exception. The dynamite that has usually been employed is real. Perhaps that is why we have such a hard time believing in the dynamite of the Sermon on the Mount. If you don't experience the healing power of the Sermon in your private life, then you can't experience it politically.

Jesus knew a great deal about God, more than any other human being. For me, he was a teacher of God. Erasmus called him the "heavenly teacher." The Sermon shows that Jesus was a teacher of great authority. Divine authority.

If you interpret the Sermon only privately or only politically, then you fail to understand Jesus' integral thinking. His gospel is as integral as his life. There is no love of God without love of humanity. To avoid any misunderstanding: the preacher of the Sermon does not mean dominion by Jesus; he means dominion by God. If you wish to emulate God, you must do "God's will." And God is love, not violence. Every person who, like the Samaritan, follows his inner voice is doing God's will. Jesus' verdict on the man who acts in his spirit is unequivocal: He will live. His verdict on the man who pays lip service to his teachings but does not act in accordance with their spirit is equally unequivocal. He is like "a foolish man who built his house upon the sand."

Why the Sermon on the Mount? It offers a chance to change the world. But the world can be changed only if we change our hearts and our ways. "Repent and believe—change the world." That was the motto of the German Catholic Conference in 1982. Official Catholicism, which often so diligently ignores the political dimension of the Sermon, was finally calling a spade a spade.

The Sermon on the Mount is more radical than the *Communist Manifesto*. Karl Marx wanted to change a few conditions, but Jesus wanted a total change of hearts.

Why the Sermon on the Mount? So long as we do not discover and understand it, we will not discover or understand our possibilities. It is the road on which every individual can become a human being, and thus all humanity can become human. Dostoevski said, "With yearning, he that I am greets him that I could be." The Sermon is not a law and not a collection of commandments. It is a promise of life, an experiment in love, a chance for humanity to become mature. Martin Buber said, "The origin of all conflict between me and my fellow man is that I do not say what I mean and do not do what I say." Why the Sermon on the Mount? Without it, not only will technology prove uncontrollable but the atomic bomb will rule over us.

The End of Creation?

For the first time in history, human beings have the possibility of ending their history. The atomic holocaust, however, would not only wipe out the 4.5 billion people alive today, it would also make billions of future lives impossible, and it would destroy the memory of all earlier life. Thus, a nuclear holocaust would be not only the death of the present, it would be the death of the future and the death of the past. It would be the death of every birth and the death of every death. Günther Anders and Jonathan Schell call the nuclear holocaust the "second death." For the first time in history, there would be no memory of earlier generations and no hope of future generations. We would kill the dead a second time, and we would hold a gun to the heads of our own children. For the first time, there would be no "partnership of the generations," in the phrase of Edmund Burke.

The crime of annihilating the people alive today would be

surpassed by the crime of annulling future generations. The wordless unborn are not included in the reckonings of the nuclear strategists. But those billions would be the decisive factor in our debit column.

Today we can destroy in just a few hours something that has taken billions of years to develop. Today—and this cannot be repeated often enough—there are more explosives per person than food. Before the Atomic Age, there was only individual death. Today, we have an idea of collective death. There have been apocalyptic moods in earlier times, but usually they were linked to God, who would destroy the world but awaken the dead. Today's apocalyptic mood is godless. Humanity has put itself into God's place. Today, human beings can put an end to creation. "The present American and Soviet arsenal, which has one million times the destructive capacity of Hiroshima, does not fulfill its purpose—one twentieth would surely be enough to guarantee the boldest deterrence theories," according to George F. Kennan.

The nuclear holocaust cannot be described in exact terms. We can only have an inkling. For it to be exactly described, there would probably be no one left to describe it. There is no surrogate earth from which the experiment of a nuclear holocaust could be calmly observed. We have no more right to experiment with the one earth than we do with human beings. Jonathan Schell, an American journalist, points out that the earth is as unique as an individual human being, and just as sacred.

Previously, further life was possible no matter how great the risk. But now, the possible annihilation of the planet Earth threatens all life.

Many people object, saying that this is only a possibility, not a certainty. Only a possibility? How many insurance policies do we take out to be forearmed against *possible* accidents? If a person understands that the possibility of an atomic holocaust can become a reality, then he has to do something. Any politics worthy of the name cannot play with creation. If we lose this game, we will not get a second chance. Even if atomic annihilation is only an intellectual possibility, this possibility must be understood politically and morally as a reality. Otherwise, we cannot hope to overcome the danger. The nuclear holocaust remains a mere possibility only if we view it as a real danger.

The only salvation is the elimination of the danger. We cannot destroy our knowledge of how to produce atomic weapons; this is something we have to live with. But the danger is too great for us to live with the weapons themselves. In the long run, an increasingly complicated nuclear technology can only bring us death. Our sole chance of survival is to deal consciously with this danger.

The atomic threat is an ecological threat, a threat to all creation. The atomic bomb is the tip of our civilization's iceberg. Civilized progress "is the result of a compensatory activity aimed at nature" (David Carver). Anything that we no longer experience naturally (sex, love, basic trust, religion) is unconsciously compensated for with a striving for money and power. The pinnacle of compensatory life is the atomic bomb. Its existence is not new, but we have repressed our sense of its danger. But anything that is repressed will sooner or later erupt.

Being human means taking part in creation. This participation is challenged by today's atomic weapons. People hope that the nuclear holocaust can be warded off with sensible actions and diplomatic agreements. But such hopes are illusory and contradict all our experience. In the Third Reich, we saw how little common sense was worth when what Hannah Arendt called the "banality of evil" was in control. We will prevent the atomic holocaust with reconciliation and love of our enemies—or we will not prevent it. The totality of all nuclear weapons expresses a gigantic, long-repressed, and long-practiced hatred such as has never been seen in human history.

Our power is destructive. We can end creation and kill everyone, but we cannot create a single human being. The fact that we cannot create even a single blade of green grass and yet refuse to recognize a Creator shows what we lack most today: self-knowledge, a sense of our limits.

Even our destructive power is borrowed. You can know the laws of nature, but that doesn't mean you make the laws. Human beings should do only one thing: preserve themselves in all modesty. If we fail to carry out this task, we shall have only everlasting darkness. There shall be no war and no peace, no hatred and no love, no sadness and no joy, no death and never again the birth of a child.

The Old Politics

*We want the end of war, we do not want war; but war can be ended
only by war; he who does not want guns must reach for a gun.*
—Mao Zedong

Annihilation or Peace?

There will probably never again be a large-scale war in Europe. In the Atomic Age, our alternative is no longer war or peace, but annihilation or peace. During wars fought before the atomic bomb, everyone could entertain the possibility of getting out alive. Today, everyone can count on dying. Yet most politicians still discuss the "war or peace" issue as though we were living in the days of General von Clausewitz, who called war "the continuation of diplomacy by other means"—a rational instrument of national politics. One country's political gain was another country's loss. Even today, many of our contemporaries are afraid of peace. Bertrand Russell has pointed out that the proudest British monuments have been erected to men like Lord Nelson or the Duke of Wellington, who were particularly skilled at killing foreigners. In the East Germany of the 1980's, soldiers are decorated for shooting and killing people trying to flee to the West.

I can sense the fear of peace in the discussions following lectures I give parallel to my work on this book. Even the tenuous rapprochement between Moscow and Peking does not inspire greater hopes for détente on the Ussuri River border. Instead, we hear anxious questions about the "strengthening of world communism." Whatever hurts the other person is good; whatever helps him is bad. So long as our relationship with the Soviet Union is dominated by this type of thinking, we can make no progress in disarmament. So long as the two superpowers hold SALT talks in order to outfox the opponent and achieve a superior position, we will have neither balance nor disarmament. So long as confrontation and not cooperation dominates the think-

ing of the two blocs, we will continue down the road to annihilation rather than the road to peace. A peace politics is possible
only when both superpowers stop using conflict for their own
gains and really attempt to end their antagonism. A policy of
peace does not aim at victory; it wants peace, compromise, and
reconciliation. Peace is like freedom. Just as freedom always
means the other person's freedom as well, so too peace means the
other person's peace. To get on the right road, someone has to
begin to abandon traditional power politics. For decades, we
have been waiting in vain for both sides to have a simultaneous
change of heart. We will wait in vain forever, even if the followers of "realpolitik" keep nurturing their superstitious faith in
this miracle. The Golden Rule of the Sermon on the Mount says
something very different: "So whatever you wish that men would
do to you, do so to them." In other words, if you want disarmament, you have to disarm yourself. And since politics usually
works very slowly, you must at least stop the arms buildup and
terminate the arms race.

A realistic peace policy means not forcing one's own will
upon the opponent and likewise not letting him force his will on
us. In the Atomic Age, we have to understand that our own
security is always identical with the opponent's security. Let's
face the facts: the Soviet SS-20 missiles are no less bad if we
oppose them with more dire weapons. Such weapons are not
lightning rods. Quite the contrary: they draw lightning. More
and more nuclear weapons on either side do not increase the
security of either side; they simply increase the danger for both.
The opponent's irrational fear of me does not get any more
rational if I try to frighten him even more. Frightening someone
has always been a condition of war. An intelligent policy would
aim at lessening the opponent's fears. "Love thy enemy" is
another term for intelligent politics.

Why does a rational policy of peace and disarmament still not have a prayer? Most people in both the East and the West put up with the armaments madness because they are uninformed. Many are uninformed because they do not wish to be informed.

"Today's sin is to be uninformed," according to Margaret Mead. Both East and West have a potential for annihilation that is one million times as strong as what destroyed Hiroshima. There are at least 15,000 nuclear warheads around the world. Jonathan Schell writes, "They grew out of history, yet they threaten to end history. They were made by men, yet they threaten to annihilate man." In his book *The Fate of the Earth,* he has compiled statements by biologists and physicians, chemists and physicists, geneticists and military men about a possible atomic holocaust. The bottom line: Today's politicians are planning the end of all life, absolute nothingness.

Georg Leber, the former West German minister of defense, has said about Schell's book: "The author's analysis is correct, but I can see no alternative to today's defense policies." We can draw little comfort from Leber's remark, considering how Schell describes the aftermath of an atomic war:

1. Radioactive dust will contaminate the entire surface of the earth.

2. Certain isotopes will emit their lethal rays for millions(!) of years.

3. The ozone layer protecting us from the sun will be partially destroyed.

4. The climate will grow cooler all over the world.

The list of the possible ways of dying is virtually endless, but a person has only one life. It doesn't say much for politicians if they can see no alternative to this possible nuclear holocaust.

Our knowledge of the aftermath is far from complete. What will become of the earth? We are only at the threshold of any knowledge. Ten years ago, we knew almost nothing about the earth sciences.

The earth and humanity can live only once. Human beings have no right to experiment with them. The aftermath of the atomic holocaust is indescribable, but the outcome is obvious: nothingness. During the past few years, United States forces have been put on red alert three times because a chip in the computerized alarm system wasn't working and once because a test tape simulating a missile attack had slipped unnoticed into the system. Human and technical errors can have a devastating impact, because each side is afraid of a first strike by the other side. In case of technical error, there is great danger that someone will abruptly order a first strike. Small comfort that this was not intended. And even smaller comfort to hear the Soviet Union constantly assert that it will never strike first. The fact is that the Soviet Union does have first-strike weapons and that it *can* use them first. Even more devastating, however, is the fact that the United States is not even willing to promise to hold back and not strike first.

According to what we know today, the world came closest to the brink of the abyss during the Cuban crisis in 1962. The Soviet Union was installing atomic missiles in Cuba, and the United States wanted to prevent this nuclear presence at its doorstep—even at the risk of atomic war! The Soviets gave in at the very last moment. The situation was summed up in Robert Kennedy's memoirs: "President Kennedy had initiated the course of events, but he no longer had control over them." A group of highly gifted statesmen made a carefully considered decision that might have led to the end of the world. Isn't it odd that such documents of a possible Armageddon could be published by a credible eyewitness, and the world did not cry out in dismay? The fact that the president of a superpower, together with four-teen staffers, can decide the fate of the earth is, I feel, both undemocratic and insane. The lack of public outcry is as shattering as the possibility of atomic war itself. The events of 1962 can recur at any time, in either Washington or Moscow. Today, it doesn't take much imagination to picture the end of mankind. But even this wee bit of imagination is lacking in many contemporaries, including most politicians.

Robert Kennedy's memoirs were published only after his assassination. His friend Theodore C. Sorensen commented: "It was Senator Robert Kennedy's intention to add a discussion of the following fundamental ethical questions: What circumstance or occasion (in case one were conceivable) could give our government or any government the moral right to bring its people and perhaps all people to the verge of nuclear annihilation?" Today, Kennedy's question is even more relevant than twenty years ago. The world has moved a bit closer to the brink; it is in greater danger of plunging into the abyss now that NATO is continuing the arms race and the Soviet Union is continuing its arms buildup in reaction. If things go on like this, either side will always find a reason for building up its arms in some sector or other. Where will all this end? How can disarmament and peaceful security ever be achieved with our current policies? As far back as 1958, C. Wright Mills wrote, "The cause of World War III will presumably be the preparation for it."

"Disarmament" policies have been pursued for over a century now. There have been dozens of "disarmament conferences." The result of this "disarmament," which has brought us closer and closer to the nuclear holocaust, has been: more and more armaments. The underlying reason for this politics of insanity is the fear of peace. The atomic holocaust is nothing but collective suicide caused by fear of peace. We are allowing weapons to settle mankind's accounts. Once the first atomic bomb has been set off, where will politicians who believed in the balance of terror get the moral grit to prevent the destruction of all life—a destruction that they have prepared so thoroughly and so expensively? In 1962, President Kennedy risked a nuclear war. Once it begins, nothing will be psychologically the same as before.

The ultimate question today is: How long can nuclear weapons protect us against nuclear weapons? Most contemporaries shield themselves against the consequences of this question by retorting with another: Aren't atom bombs the very thing that has prevented war in Europe during the past four decades? When during the past two centuries has there ever been such a long peace in Europe as after 1945?

Putting Off the Deadline

It may be true that the existence of the atomic bomb has prevented war for a time. I find it more likely, however, that atomic bombs have merely delayed World War III. The last few years prove that a great many matters have piled up behind the "atomic shield." If we're lucky, then the atomic machine has at best offered the earth a few moments' grace in putting off the deadline—until the almost inevitable human or technical failure that will bring annihilation.

The period of grace might be shortened, since a dozen governments will have atomic weapons by the end of this decade. And others will follow. Things can't go on for long when $700 billion dollars a year are spent on armaments, while a million human beings starve to death in the same period. Everything has its consequences. At some point, every starving child will demand his due. Imagine what would happen if the Idi Amins of the world had atomic weapons, if, as in 1962, a supposedly responsible and cautious statesman like Kennedy took the risk. It is questionable whether we can prevent the further spread of nuclear weapons. It is certain, however, that we will not prevent it so long as the superpowers themselves have atomic weapons. So long as anyone has them, everything can only get worse.

In 1968, Robert S. McNamara wrote, "Assured annihilation is the very essence of the whole deterrence concept." Thus, the destructive intention has to be credible, and annihilation has to be "guaranteed." The current military doctrines of both blocs remind me of a statement made by an American general during the war in Vietnam after he ordered the destruction of a village. "I had to destroy this village in order to protect it from the Communists." The threatened annihilation has to be credible. Both sides are extremely well prepared. If push comes to shove, we will have the means for national defense, but no nation to defend.

Until now, we thought it made sense to intimidate an opponent by threatening to use atomic weapons. But what if the opponent won't be intimidated? The doctrine is supposed to be credible, but the deed would be unjustifiable. The contradiction remains unresolved. Since the nuclear holocaust would strike everyone, the distinction between friendly and hostile atomic powers would be meaningless. Not only the annihilation of mankind but the very theory of its annihilation is unacceptable.

On World Peace Day of 1983, Pope John Paul II said that we must eliminate not only "every war, but everything that can lead to war." The pope is against any kind of arms buildup. Our unbridled reason prevents such insights. Descartes' conclusion, "I think, therefore I am," has led us astray. Our rationality has to take a few lessons from our emotions and intuitions in order to imagine survival and learn peace. Neither life nor permanent love can thrive on the brink of nothingness. Perhaps people are now asking so intensely about the meaning of life because its meaning—that is, life itself—is being threatened. And if people see no meaning in life, then they see no meaning in love. Love relationships are getting shorter, just as the survival deadline keeps drawing nearer. Today's younger generation, which has not spent a day without atomic weapons, is under mental stress like no earlier generation. Perhaps that is the reason for the No Future philosophy. If you can't hope for survival, then you can't hope. Earlier generations had time. The atomic generation has to fight for its time. They have to be "agriculturalists of time" (Jonathan Schell) and cultivate their future years. Perhaps this is how we can learn to live and survive as one humanity.

God's commandment "Thou shalt not kill" must now be understood in new terms. You have to allow future generations to live. You have to allow them to be born. The present generation has parental obligations toward posterity. Parents do not put their children in straitjackets; parents love their children.

If talks about intimidation are honest, then at some point the advocates of intimidation are forced to admit that they must, if necessary, be prepared to annihilate mankind for the sake of national sovereignty, even though this means that the nation too will be wiped out. Likewise, the advocates of total disarmament have to admit that their suggestions are not compatible with national sovereignty. Today, many people who use the term "national sovereignty" are really talking about oil. Others say "socialism" instead of "sovereignty," but they are really talking about their power. These are the "vital interests" for whose sake the political leaders threaten to wage war.

Our ideologies of socialism and capitalism have had their day. Now, the primary goal is survival together. What is more important: oil and socialism or life? If you want to maintain the old politics, with war as the ultimate means, during the Atomic Age, then you risk annihilating all human life. Faced with the possibility of nuclear holocaust, our political realism becomes biological nihilism. Technically, atomic war is only possible, but we are forced to accept this possibility as certain if we are to prevent the nuclear holocaust. The fundamental contradiction is that we use the threat of annihilation in order to escape annihilation. This may work for a while. But ultimately it leads only to annihilation. There is a law of history: Whenever too many guns get together, they always start shooting. That is a lesson we have learned from the past. Our task is not to forget or suppress history, but to remember it.

If it turns out that we remain unable to practice military nonviolence in the Atomic Era, then mankind will have no future. The questions emerging from this insight are not pleasant, but this is no reason not to ask them. Jonathan Schell writes, "It may be only by descending into this hell in imagination now that we can hope to escape descending into it in reality at some later time." The knowledge we have to acquire about a possible nuclear holocaust is, by itself, no protection against it. But without this knowledge, there can be no hope. We have to understand that an atomic war will leave no winners and no losers, just corpses. Only the weapons would win. Today, all human beings are hostages of nuclear weapons. The Eastern bloc nations are hostages of Western weapons, and the Western nations are hostages of Eastern weapons. Southern nations are the hostages of both East and West. Disarmament talks will remain futile so long as the negotiators fail to understand that they are the hostages of their own atomic bombs. Most of the nuclear-freeze proposals that were made at Geneva in 1982 seem to be based on a *single* point of view: they are or appear to be unacceptable to the other side.

For a long time, we unconsciously rebelled against being hostages. Our souls became ill. We have less trust in ourselves, in others, and in the future than earlier generations did. If you trust in bombs, then you will lose your trust in human beings.

Missiles Are Magnets

If the United States keeps stationing arms in Western Europe and if the Soviets refuse to dismantle their SS-20's, then both sides will confirm the sarcastic remark that the "Americans and Russians are bravely determined to defend themselves down to the last European."

In December 1982, it became known that the United States would transfer the NATO headquarters in Stuttgart to London in case of an emergency. Such a plan may be strategically correct, but it does not contribute to easing the fears of the people involved, especially since nothing was said about transferring them.

Once again, we were shown that the United States makes important military decisions without consulting its allies. The Western superpower ignored West Germany in regard to building the neutron bomb, the theory of limited atomic warfare, and the possible transfer of NATO headquarters. This indifference feeds the suspicion that, for some American political leaders, West Germany would be something like a "throwaway Cuba" in an emergency.

The nonstop arms buildup makes both East and West Germany the starting point for an atomic war limited to Europe. The American cruise missiles and Pershing II's will be the targets of the Soviet SS-20's, and vice versa. Thus, atomic defense will become defense unto death. It cannot be in Germany's best interests to serve as an atomic launching pad for the United States and an atomic target for the Soviet Union. The Soviet middle-range missiles are already dangerous enough. And they will become even more dangerous because of the buildup of Western middle-range missiles. The Pershing II's and cruise missiles do not deflect lightning; they attract it. The same is true of the Soviet SS-20's, as demonstrated by the Western arms buildup. Even in peacetime, the Eastern and Western missiles attract one another like magnets. This increases the overall danger. The nuclear development proves that the watchword of the 1950's peace movement was correct: "Missiles are magnets." That's the way it has been, and that's the way it will always be— until someone starts to halt and go back. Only then will we have a chance for *dis*armament pressure, instead of our previous armaments pressure.

In our present system of intimidation, each side needs its buildup—more and more arms. However, this development cannot go on with impunity. Sooner or later, the big bang has to come. It has always come, as far back as we can remember. Continuing the arms buildup in this situation means making the catastrophe more probable. Cruise missiles and Pershing II's can reach the Soviet Union in just minutes and wipe out more lives in a few moments than Hitler's armies did in six years. We can assume that the Soviet Union will react just as irrationally as the West is reacting to the SS-20's. The arms buildup is a process of fighting fire with fire.

Since the warning period for Pershing II's and cruise missiles will last only four to six minutes, the Soviet Union prefers having a computer respond to the Western arms buildup. Given our previous experience, a few Russian negotiators point out, the brief warning period is not long enough for human brains and hands. According to our knowledge of technical errors in military computers, four to six minutes are not always enough for Americans to catch a mistake. *Thus, we are now automating the ultimate decision on life and death.* If we continue the arms race, we will be suspending our lives from the silken threads of a computer.

Kindergarten Reflexes in Politics

In their nuclear policies, the two superpowers are of the same flesh and the same spirit. Each side is doing the very thing that it reproaches the other for. Each side is justifying its own sins with the sins of the other. In the Third World too, American policies after Jimmy Carter's presidency have become more and more "Soviet." Washington threatens to intervene in Nicaragua. Each superpower refuses to do what it demands of the other. Many right-wing Germans are defending the American nuclear rockets, and many left-wing Germans are defending the Soviet equivalents. The West German Communist Party, which is involved in the peace movement, opposes the NATO arms buildup, yet defends the Soviet SS-20's. The party's motto is: "Create peace without NATO weapons."

After 1945, the Soviet Union had a vast superiority in conventional weapons in Europe. At that time, the United States began its nuclear preparations. By the 1970's, the Soviet Union could match the American arsenal. Today, most politicians and military men talk of an approximate balance. The United States is superior in quality, the Soviet Union in quantity. Yet each side keeps finding it has some new point of vulnerability. If you want total security in the Atomic Era, you have to reckon with total annihilation. Politicians call this policy rational and speak of "objective atomic pressures." And indeed, the atomic bomb has been pressuring us for a long time—which is probably the most irrational policy that human beings have ever maintained on this globe. Perhaps atomic bombs did prevent European wars for a time. But sooner or later, there is a deadline. If the arms race can't be halted, if a dozen governments have nuclear bombs by the end of the 1980's and perhaps fifty governments by the year 2000, then world peace is more precarious than at any time since 1945. Not because mankind has become worse since 1945 or since the Middle Ages or since antiquity, but because for the first time in history, mankind has the means to self-destruct. Man has "far more effective ways of confirming his wickedness," wrote C. G. Jung.

Our knowledge has increased, but our ethics have lagged behind. Historically, this disparity is due to the Enlightenment, of which all our liberals are so proud. In reality, however, our rationality has not been emancipated, it has merely been divorced from responsibility, emotion, religion, and intuition. Since the Middle Ages, science and technology have progressed by leaps and bounds; yet we know less about the human soul than our forebears, who at least had an awareness of sin. The Enlightenment idolized reason. *The atomic dead end is the dead end of our separated reason.* We are not integrally human, but unilaterally "rational." The results are well known. We are now on the brink. Yet we are still not aware of the full scope of the situation. Is it really rational to be able to kill all mankind several times and yet to keep manufacturing more and more weapons? Even the planned NATO arms buildup is no longer rationalized by security, since many people no longer believe this pretext. Instead, politicians cite the weapons of the other side—and this argument is taken seriously by many.

If more weapons are to be produced because the other side has them too, then this policy is a kindergarten reflex. If this metaphor is offensive, it is more insulting to children than to politicians. In any event, the outcome of this policy is not greater security, but greater insecurity. The end of this deification of reason and science would be the beginning of a new knowledge, an awareness that only a change of heart and a new sense of responsibility can help us now. Nothing proves to be as irrational as pure reason. It is neither pure nor reasonable. In the

Atomic Era, knowledge without conscience wrecks not only the soul but also life.

The American National Conference of Catholic Bishops declared in the summer of 1982: "We consider it immoral even to *threaten* with the use of such weapons." U.S. Secretary of Defense Caspar Weinberger has called this position "dangerous." Yet more and more American bishops are joining the international Catholic peace movement, the Pax Christi (Peace of Christ). They are thus emphasizing their opposition to the Pax Americana of their government. One can no more identify Western capitalism with liberty than Eastern communism with fraternity. People in Western countries may have more freedom than the citizens of Eastern Europe. But the question is: *Are* we truly more free; do we *live* more freely if we too allow our governments to pursue the same nuclear madness that we condemn in the Soviet Union?

Pax Christi: the politics of the Sermon on the Mount. This is a farewell to the Pax Americana and the Pax Sovietica.

Politicians without Self-Knowledge

Many politicians do not shed light on their nuclear policies. Instead, they numb their own and other people's minds. In 1981, John F. Lehman, U.S. secretary of the navy, named a nuclear submarine *Corpus Christi*, after the city of that name in Texas. When the sub was launched, he said, "Educated in the teachings of the church, I am particularly aware that military power is viewed by the church as an instrument of peace."

Lehman overlooked the fact that today the Catholic Church is trying to remind the United States of the Sermon on the Mount. When the American bishops' conference protested against this incomprehensible blasphemy, the vessel was renamed *City of Corpus Christi*. In November 1982, Ronald Reagan called the planned MX missiles "peacekeepers." Pacifist missiles! These euphemistic names conceal the fact that each of the 100 MX missiles has the destructive power of 175 Hiroshima bombs. The underlying attitude is not ill will, but something far more dangerous, because it does not even cause pangs of conscience. Many politicians no longer know what they are doing and what they are helping to prepare. Talking and talking and never taking time to read or think or meditate, they lack self-knowledge. They condemn the other side for doing what they themselves then do. For instance, building nuclear bombs. They turn the Golden Rule of the Sermon on the Mount upside down. The ethical authority of their consciences remains on a conscious level. Depth psychology long ago pointed out the existence of the subconscious. Most politicians are unconscious of the fact that they are preparing for war. While planning destruction more and more precisely, they keep talking more and more about peace. In politics, however, the unconscious, especially our unconscious evil, is deliberately omitted. No one wants to know about it. This is obvious in nearly all election speeches. In these speeches, as in the general East–West conflict, all wicked things are projected upon an external enemy in order (seemingly) to exculpate the internal enemy. The external enemy is then reproached for everything that we ourselves keep doing.

Often, politicians have no sense of the consequences of their decisions and reject any personal responsibility for them. And often they appear to be glad that they have no self-knowledge. Thus, no unpleasant thought disturbs the shimmer of their illusions. They too feel that he who is without sin should cast the first stone. I do not wish to judge; I merely wish to point out what a person will become conscious of when he begins to comprehend the politics of the Sermon on the Mount. Knowledge of the existence of the unconscious is indispensable for all true self-knowledge and self-contemplation. Only the deployment of the unconscious allows us to move "from the limited ego to the vaster self" (C. G. Jung) and on to self-knowledge. Self-knowledge is the life goal of every person. Yet today's politicians do not take the time to increase their self-knowledge—to think, read, meditate, pray. And we no longer know or believe what our dreams can contribute to our self-knowledge night after night. Unlike certain primitive peoples, we have no antenna for these nocturnal gifts from within us. Liberated from the random and manipulable character of the conscious mind, our dreams lead us through the strata of our subconscious. Dream analysis can give us this happy experience, so that we may then have greater understanding of ourselves and others.

New knowledge demands new ethical decisions. Illusions are often a more convenient and (especially in politics) frivolous alibi, helping us to shirk ethical consequences. If you don't know yourself, you won't recognize your own responsibility in conflicts. You will only seek the speck in your brother's eye. Jesus shows us the opposite road: "Take the log out of your own eye." "Judge not." "So whatever you wish that men would do to you, do so to them."

Jesus does not demand blind obedience. Following him means taking the road of self-knowledge to reach the freedom of ethical decisions. The ethics of the Sermon on the Mount has nothing to do with moral prescriptions or the letter of the law. It involves self-knowledge, truthfulness, and freedom.

Living under the threat of nuclear holocaust, we must keep one thing in mind: A person is capable of politics if he is capable of disarming. Granted, if we apply this criterion, there are few real politicians.

Or can we pin our hopes on SALT talks? So far, every disarmament conference has been anything but disarming. Politicians used the word *disarmament* to mean their own military advantage. "This time, I'm optimistic," Helmut Kohl says over and over again. I find his optimism more and more puzzling. Optimism as a principle can be an illness, just like pessimism. Given the horrible facts, the only helpful and permissible stance one can take is analytical skepticism. Believing that something can't exist if it shouldn't exist, many German democrats and churchmen deceived themselves during the 1930's. The results were disastrous. But this time, we won't be roused from our illusions. This time, the horror won't last for twelve years. It will all be over in a few hours or days.

In Geneva, the negotiators on both sides were hawks. I cannot imagine that such negotiations can bring us any closer to a disarmament worthy of the name. The Geneva talks are like the efforts of two umpires to agree on ending soccer because the number of fouls keeps increasing. They may work out the most complicated rules, but they will not succeed in abolishing soccer.

The arms talks were conducted in such a way that each propaganda apparatus could easily blame the other side for its own failure. In late 1982, both superpowers already claimed that the other was not in earnest about negotiating. Although more and more people can see through this pass-the-buck diplomacy, most politicians keep rehashing the same old argument: *The best way to prevent the catastrophe is to prepare oneself more and more carefully.* Nothing productive could be achieved in Geneva. Each side talked about disarmament, but meant that of the other side. This game has been going on for decades.

Every Second Is a World War

It was not until he left politics in January 1981 that Jimmy Carter admitted that the danger of atomic war is growing. "And since other governments are obtaining these weapons, it is only a question of time before madness, despair, greed, or miscalculation will release this terrible power." An American president leaving office must know what he's talking about when he says, "In a worldwide nuclear war, more destructive power would be released in a single second than in the entire Second World War."

If one nevertheless advocates escalating the arms buildup and believes that atomic weapons will guarantee security, can he still have faith, hope, and love in the spirit of the Sermon on the Mount? The new aspect of the present-day arms systems is that the adversary fears them because they are first-strike weapons and acts accordingly. He improves his own first-strike weapons, making them faster and faster, more and more accurate, more and more efficient. This heightens the danger of war. First-strike weapons, as many informed commentators have noted, offer a great temptation to use them "in time": Such a system cannot remain stable in a crisis. First-strike weapons are for waging war, not preventing it.

So far, as we have always been told, atomic weapons were supposed to prevent war. But now, they are to be used for fighting and of course winning a war. So far, atomic weapons could be politically justified. Now, they are being "militarized."

So long as atomic weapons were a deterrent, the logical consequence was the "balance of terror." But if atomic weapons are to be used in war, then each government is forced to strive for superiority. Unless governments stop moving in this direction, they can neither stop the arms buildup nor disarm. Before, military superiority was unimportant. Now, it is necessary. This is the new and the real danger.

The Falklands War proved once again that the primary maxim in today's foreign policy is not the prevention of war, but so-called national sovereignty and preservation of power—with military means when necessary. If an operetta war was fought over the Falklands, then how much greater is the danger of war over Berlin, the Indian–Pakistani border, or economic interests in the Middle East? Nuclear first-strike weapons will make future crises a lot more dangerous than earlier ones. Any international crisis can trigger the nuclear holocaust. If a government can launch the first nuclear missile, it will do so in order to anticipate the enemy. Thus, the politics of first-strike weapons makes attack appear the only form of "defense." The crazy thing about our present situation is that an atomic war can be started not by aggressions, but by a mere desire to survive. And who would not wish to survive if he felt he were being attacked? Does any American or Soviet political leader so much as hint in a foreign-policy speech that he does *not* feel threatened? If the atomic holocaust is looming, then there are only two possibilities. We can halt the arms race, as demanded by the American freeze movement. Or we can prepare for nuclear war, which is what both Moscow and Washington are now doing.

The Annihilation of the Enemy

Caspar Weinberger spoke to the Council on Foreign Relations on June 18, 1981: "If intimidation fails, then we have to be able to win in order to survive."

Prior to the Reagan Administration, American politicians always justified nuclear weapons as "deterrents," as means of "intimidation." But now, they are to be used in nuclear warfare with the aim of annihilating the enemy. The same goal was announced by Premier Leonid Brezhnev on November 7, 1982, shortly before his death. He used the special lingo of all peace politicians: "The essence of our politics is love of peace. . . . The potential aggressor should know that we shall irrevocably strike back and wipe him out." Yuri Andropov carried on the policies of his predecessor, and Konstantin Chernenko has inherited them from Andropov.

According to the official emergency plans of the United

States, 80 percent of the population has a chance of surviving a nuclear war; 45 million Americans will die. If 20 percent are to perish, how many people would survive in Europe, the main battlefield? The American government feels that seven days would be enough to evacuate its major cities. Once the evacuation began, wouldn't the Soviet Union feel compelled to strike first, rather than waiting passively for the United States to make the first move? An attempt at preparing for an atomic war can bring it about.

The most important question is: What will happen when intimidation fails? The representatives of both superpowers offer a clear-cut answer: nuclear war. They disagree merely on the scope of annihilation. "Only" 45 million Americans among the hundreds of millions or more of corpses?

Franz König, cardinal of Vienna, has little solace for any possible survivors: "The living will envy the dead." Whenever the two superpowers talk about disarmament, they mean the other side's disarmament. And whenever they talk about security, they usually mean their own security. And whenever they talk about balance, they mean their own superiority. Doesn't the unlimited construction of SS-20 bases prove that the Soviets are trying to achieve a superior position so that they can pressure the West? And doesn't the American intention to produce 17,000 nuclear warheads in this decade demonstrate the same striving to have the upper hand?

The balance of terror stopped being a political possibility the moment the negotiating parties failed to agree on what balance means. Three days before his death, Brezhnev told the Soviet generals, "You will have to march very far." What does that mean in the nuclear era? Both sides use the word *balance* to mean superiority. Both sides use the term *arms buildup* to mean war preparations. Since the United States is economically far superior to the Soviet Union, there is greater and greater danger that the Western superpower will use this superiority on a military level, and the Eastern superpower will desperately try to strike first while it believes it still has a chance. Carl Friedrich von Weizsäcker says, "If you drive the Russian bear into a corner, there is a great danger that he will pounce." And this means: on the atomic battlefield known as Europe. The West often fails to see that the Soviet Union faces four nuclear powers all by itself: the United States, France, England, and China.

In the summer of 1982, the *Los Angeles Times* wrote about a "strategic general plan" that the American government had drawn up for a lengthy nuclear war. When Secretary of Defense Weinberger reacted to this story by sending a letter to forty newspapers, he described the general military and political principles of NATO, but he did not take a clear-cut position on this plan, much less deny its existence. Evidently, the United States has plans for lengthy atomic warfare. After all, President Reagan has said that he can imagine a nuclear conflict limited to Europe. Weinberger talks of the "possibility of a response that permits survival." In his letter, the secretary of defense points out that there are no winners in an atomic war. Yet several weeks earlier, in an address at the Naval War College, he had stated, "Successful intimidation demands responsible and effective contingency plans in case deterrence fails and we are attacked. In these plans, we do not plan to lose." Thus, there are plans for waging and winning a nuclear war!

The London *Times* commented on Weinberger's contradictory remarks: "The danger is that an American president who attempts to convince the Russians that he views an atomic war as conceivable and winnable, will ultimately convince himself, especially if he regards the Soviet Union with profound hostility. This could tempt him to take risks that he would otherwise avoid." If Reagan actually managed to convince the Soviet Union that the United States would have nuclear superiority within the foreseeable future, then would there not be a great danger that the Soviet leaders might suddenly believe they ought to prevent American superiority as long as they can? According to the prevalent philosophy of war, this goal could be reached only by means of an atomic war.

Caspar Weinberger assumes that the Soviet Union is preparing for a nuclear war and that it believes it could win. In his reply in the German newspaper *Die Zeit*, Theo Sommer tersely asks the American secretary of defense: "Even if the Soviets actually prepare fully and intend to do what you assume they might do, what good would it do to imitate their follies?" Shortly after Reagan took office, Weinberger had told the House Budget Committee, "This administration will increase our military potential so greatly that it can prevent the Soviet Union from waging a world war or wage one itself." Or wage one itself!

Around that time, Eugene Rostow was asked by the U.S. Senate's Foreign Relations Committee whether a country could survive nuclear attack. He replied that Japan had not only survived nuclear attack, but actually flourished afterward! And Rostow was chairman of the official national agency charged with responsibility for arms control and disarmament!

If you can imagine a limited atomic war, then the thought of nuclear attack is not terrifying—so long as you live outside its limits. To many Eastern and Western Europeans, those comments by U.S. politicians sound a lot more threatening than to North Americans. Even more threatening to Western Europeans are the Soviet SS-20 rockets, because they increase the possibility of a limited nuclear war. Today, no politician wants an atomic war. At least, so we assume! But there are politicians in Moscow and Washington who are ready to use atomic weapons if they feel threatened. Even if the danger of war does not seem to increase objectively, the fear of this danger keeps growing on both sides because of the arms buildup and the arms race. And both sides are becoming more and more willing to react to the danger with atomic weapons.

If an atomic war is started, we may assume that the participants would prefer to keep it limited. But here, too, the question is: Could they really keep it limited? The most vulnerable country would be Germany, a divided land, with the highest number of nuclear weapons on both sides of the Iron Curtain. For Germans, a limited nuclear war must be inconceivable; once it begins, nothing will remain the same. The belligerents would launch more and more weapons—as planned. The destruction would never halt, because each side would try to anticipate the other. And both sides have already made sure that annihilation will be total. Politicians who have planned and "tested" total nuclear war will not hesitate to put their plans into action if they feel that they or their power is threatened. In Vietnam, the United States kept fighting long after it made no military sense to do so. The Soviets occupied Afghanistan, claiming they had to protect it against "imperialism." The American crimes in Vietnam no more justify Soviet nuclear arms than the Soviet crimes in Afghanistan justify American nuclear arms. When Leonid Brezhnev died, our situation suddenly became very clear. Ronald Reagan assured the world that the United States wants peace, but only from a position of strength. And Yuri Andropov replied the next day that the Soviet Union wants peace, but only from a position of strength.

For both sides, *strength* is just another word for the arms buildup: more arms, first-strike arms, war preparations. For both the American and the Soviet leadership, strength is the sum total of a country's capacity to annihilate. So far, arms talks have been the opium of people asking for a nuclear freeze. These negotiations have served merely as placebos. The politics of strength can lead only to more confrontation, never to cooperation. "We want the end of war, we do not want war; but war can be ended only by war; he who does not want guns must reach for a gun" (Mao Zedong). That is the old politics of strength. Such policies have almost always led to war. And almost all wars are justified as ways of achieving peace. It is on the basis of this philosophy of strength ("I'll do unto you before you do unto me") that the superpowers have negotiated in Geneva—and gotten nowhere—for decades. War has not been abolished. Instead, the danger of war has grown into the danger of annihilation. The outcome of every disarmament conference has been a greater arms buildup. This has been going on for over a century.

In 1932, the German diplomat Ernst Baron von Weizsäcker took part in a disarmament conference in Geneva. One year *earlier*, he had noted, "One thing is certain about the prospects of the disarmament conference: There will be no real reduction of arms." Long before the talks began, von Weizsäcker called the conference "the planned disarmament lie."

Nothing contradicts the spirit of the Sermon on the Mount or real life more than thinking and acting in terms of strength. Hitherto, nuclear weapons seemed to prevent a war in Europe. But now it is more and more obvious that a nuclear war has merely been put on hold. Annihilation begins with words.

Is Helmut Kohl against the Arms Buildup?

West German Chancellor Helmut Kohl said in a speech on October 13, 1982, "To create peace without weapons: This is an understandable wish, and it is also a highly dangerous illusion. To create peace only with weapons: This would be a deadly blindness. To create peace with fewer and fewer weapons: This is the mission of our time."

I agree with him. This is a road to disarmament. If you consider this the correct road, then you must take it. The road and the goal are identical here. Yet only a few sentences further, the chancellor contradicted himself: "The government of the Federal Republic of Germany agrees absolutely with the double resolution of NATO in 1979, which offers negotiations on reducing and limiting Soviet and American middle-range nuclear systems. Our government will carry out these resolutions and advocate them domestically: the negotiation portion and—if necessary—the arms-building portion."

If you feel that the "mission of our time" is to "create peace with fewer and fewer weapons," then you cannot continue the arms race. For a buildup of arms means *more* arms.

West Germany began preparing for an arms buildup in late 1982. In the election of 1983, both Helmut Kohl and his predecessor, Helmut Schmidt, supported the double resolution. Now, the arms buildup continues. The Soviet Union is deploying new missiles in East Germany and Czechoslovakia, and the United States has responded in kind with nuclear missiles sited in Britain. We keep getting closer and closer to the atomic holocaust, a frighteningly inevitable result.

"I saw that Hiroshima had disappeared," said a history professor from Hiroshima on the day of the explosion. In the Atomic Age, every moment can be our last. The professor's experience on August 6, 1945, can be mankind's experience tomorrow. Except that after the global holocaust, no life would be left on earth, just deadly silence everywhere, complete nothingness. As I write these lines, I cannot be altogether certain that they will actually be printed. And once they are printed, there is no assurance that they can be read. Prior to August 1945, a Japanese would probably have waved off such thoughts, as we do today. We live as if we knew nothing. But can a society be considered mentally sound if it closes its eyes to the possibility of its own annihilation?

Politicians try to calm our fears. Fear, they tell us, is not a good adviser for the future. The point is: Do we have reasons to be afraid? Unfounded fear makes you sick. Well-founded fear is wholesome. The fear of the atomic holocaust is well founded. It is therefore the best adviser for the future. The person who thinks and has an imagination is haunted by his fear of the tremendous destructive power of the bomb. We can open our eyes only if we perceive this well-founded fear, so that we will not walk blindly toward the brink. When the bombs were dropped on Hiroshima and Nagasaki, mankind lost its atomic innocence. Today, we have over 20,000 megatons of nuclear explosive power, and more are added every day. We really should know what's what. In *Pedagogy of the Atomic Age*, Peter Kern and Hans Georg Wittig used a vivid simile to demonstrate nuclear development since 1945. The combined nuclear destructive capacity of East and West is 1.6 million times more powerful than the bomb dropped on Hiroshima; this is the same ratio as that "between the thickness of a pencil and the altitude of Mount Everest." In 1976, Carl Friedrich von Weizsäcker said, "World War III is probable." During the 1970's, West Germany became agitated and even panicky because of a few dozen terrorists. Yet almost no one was bothered by the forecast made by a renowned German peace researcher that a nuclear war was a likelihood.

A third world war without atomic weapons is out of the question. In the preatomic age, a person who wrote or engaged in politics had something to look forward to; he could be sure that his work had a future. This gave his activities a deeper meaning. The same thing is felt—usually unconsciously—by mothers and fathers and all people who would like to be parents. Many people wonder whether we should still have children in the Atomic Age. Yes, we should! Children are a powerful trump of hope, an affirmation of life and a negation of the increasing militarization of our lives. I did not have my children so that they would burn up in atomic lightning or live their lives in terror of nuclear weapons. Today, the meaning of anything we do is more questionable. Deadlines are approaching. People are getting more and more impatient. These are the psychological consequences of the Atomic Era, and we are barely aware of them.

In the past, when people thought about death, they knew they would survive in the memories of others. Today, we no longer have this comfort. We no longer know whether or how long anyone will go on living. If the manner of death becomes absurd, then doesn't the manner of life become absurd? Are young people so scared of life because old people are so scared of death? Our leaders have many good reasons for stopping the arms buildup. They ought to act on them.

With Norbert Blüm in East Germany

In September 1982, I experienced at first hand the difficulties politicians have with peace policies. A few days before Norbert Blüm became a member of the West German cabinet, we spent a few days privately in East Germany. We wanted to find out about the peace movement there, but we kept arguing about peace. In East Berlin, we talked with Professor Herbert Häber of the Politburo of East Germany's Socialist Unity Party. "You can always count on my support if you're against the NATO arms buildup," I told Häber, a Communist. "But it would help if you gave your comrades in Moscow a piece of your mind about the SS-20 missiles." Häber and Blüm used the same arguments to defend the atomic systems in their respective countries. Each accused the other of continuing the arms race. The Communist spoke about Western superiority in long-range missiles, and the other spoke about Eastern superiority in middle-range missiles. One man's SS-20's were the other man's MX's. The discussion was dominated by arms technology and weapon initials. No one mentioned the threatened people and nations. I am convinced that understanding between nations cannot be achieved by military technology. A true rapport between today's blocs can be achieved only when one stops trying to intimidate the other. If you keep arming, you keep intimidating; if you disarm, you stop intimidating.

Naturally, both Häber and Blüm were all for peace and disarmament. But each said that the other had kept building up and that he had to be the first to disarm. When I stuck to my guns and insisted that both the East and the West ought to stop arming, independently of what the other side did, I had both politicians against me. This was an important experience for me. I now realized that politicians are unable to attain a nuclear freeze chiefly because they are frightened of disarming and ultimately frightened of peace. Their image of the enemy is so deeply rooted that they are no longer aware of it. Naturally, no one cares to admit it, but it's true. Each side needs the other as its enemy. This applies as much to my friend Norbert Blüm as it does to the worthy member of the Socialist Unity Party in East Germany.

Nothing is so difficult for a human being as to make himself aware of things that prevent us from becoming more human. Bertrand Russell used a nice example to describe the politicians' fear of peace: 'I once had a donkey who was quartered in a stall. The stall caught fire. Several strong men had to struggle with the donkey in order to drag him to safety. Had he been left to himself, his terror would have assured his death by fire. The situation of the great powers today is very similar. And that is particularly so when we come to the question of disarmament." The blinded donkey ignored what was best for him. He was blind to the deadly danger. Many politicians are likewise so blinded by hatred that they cannot see the common enemy, the atomic bomb. Their hearts are blind.

Before meeting with Häber, Blüm and I visited Rainer Eppelmann, a Protestant minister in East Berlin. Shortly before Robert Havemann's death, these two men had composed the *Berlin Appeal: Create Peace without Weapons.* Young Eppelmann and old Havemann are the midwives of the East German peace movement. The issue brought together the idealistic Christian Eppelmann and the humanistic Communist Havemann. The West German peace movement uses the slogan: "What if they gave a war and nobody came?" Eppelmann painted the following words on his garage door: "Just suppose—what if peace comes, and people at the top just don't notice?"

Neither Reagan nor Chernenko, neither the West German nor the East German chancellor, neither Blüm nor Häber wants war. But that doesn't mean very much. Albert Einstein said, "It's easy to praise peace, but it's useless. What we need is active participation in the struggle against war and everything that leads to war."

Nearly all politicians who have waged war have been in favor of peace. Most wars have been unwanted, yet they have been waged. Hitler was an exception—he wanted war. Our language reveals that we do not make anyone responsible for wars; they simply "break out." We talk about wars as if they were natural catastrophes or strokes of fate inflicted on human beings by some higher power.

It doesn't matter what politicians say about peace. The only thing that counts is what politicians *do* about peace.

Everyone Talks about Disarming

The word *really* is always a dead giveaway in the vocabulary of politicians on either side of the Iron Curtain. Everyone *really* wants disarmament. But "the Communists," "the capitalists," "our armed forces," and the constantly cited "pressures of reality" continue to prevent politicians from putting their money where their mouths are. Now, if the atomic reality pressures us to do things that we do not *really* want to do, then we will have war forced upon us sooner or later—a war that we naturally and *really* didn't want. The Soviets *really* want a nuclear freeze, and the United States *really* wants a nuclear freeze. Yet they keep increasing their nuclear arsenals. Pointing to the other side, each side does what it condemns the other for doing. I don't actually know which side has a few more missiles. But I do know that this slight margin hasn't mattered for a long time. If each side can kill the other a dozen times, then *any* form of arms buildup is absurd. And the rationales that Eastern and Western experts come up with are anything but convincing. There is no way to justify the preparations for the destruction of mankind and its planet. The threat of annihilation is, without any doubt, contrary to the spirit of the Sermon on the Mount. The atomic bombs in the Soviet Union are no less dangerous because they are balanced by new atomic bombs in the United States. The nuclear policies of either side keep reflecting those of the other. Soviet bombs threaten humanity as much as American bombs. Both superpowers are lighting the fuse of one and the same atomic powder keg, which threatens one and the same world. Both superpowers can wipe out mankind.

If the arms buildup continues despite everything, then more and more West Germans will desert NATO in their minds, just as more and more East Germans will desert the Warsaw Pact in their minds, if the Soviets do not remove their SS-20's. Abandoning the bloc ideology is the only thing that can save Germany from becoming a shooting range for the superpowers. The atomic powder keg that we are sitting on has two holes: one in the East and one in the West. If the East keeps adding more explosives, then the West feels it has to do likewise, and vice versa. This situation cannot go on. I no longer trust the infallibility of those who say, "We have everything under control." I now trust in their fallibility. If a politician wants to keep up the arms race despite the nuclear vulnerability of our world, then he no longer deserves our trust. Helmut Gollwitzer says, "If a man sleeps on a powder keg, then he shares the responsibility when it finally blows up and destroys all life. If a man stands up and lends a hand in getting rid of the powder keg, he is putting into practice the message of Easter."

Shortly before returning to West Germany, Norbert Blüm and I visited Bishop Werner Krusche in the East German town of Magdeburg. He described the fight the Protestant Church in East Germany has been waging against nuclear arms. It now fully dawned on me whom the arms race is really aimed at: not just the Kremlin leaders and the East German leaders, but also the millions of Eastern Europeans, who yearn for peace as deeply as we do. Our arms buildup is aimed at millions of Protestants in East Germany, millions of Catholics in Poland, millions of Orthodox Christians in the Soviet Union, as well as millions of atheists. We are pointing atomic rockets at millions of human beings who want peace as much as we do. Can we still claim credibility if we carry on about human rights in Eastern Europe, yet threaten to wipe out Eastern Europe with our nuclear weapons? We fail to see that our plans for defending freedom could lead to annihilating millions of people.

By wiping them out, we hope to destroy a system that is hostile to us and suppresses them. First, the tyrannical system took away their rights. Now we threaten to take away their lives—in the name of freedom!

A politics of intimidation cannot guarantee protection in case of attack. It can only guarantee that millions of people will be wiped out if we are wiped out. Neither defense nor salvation can be counted on, only annihilation. We want to prevent annihilation by preparing for and threatening annihilation. Yet our threats keep producing more threats from the adversary. The paradox is insoluble. This doctrine does not get rid of the bombs; we merely internalize them. We are starting to believe in them.

Are we in the West truly free if we do not resist all further escalation of atomic weapons—for our sake, and also for the sake of Eastern Europeans, who need a lot more courage than we to protest against the nuclear madness of their leaders?

Fear of Peace

One reason I am writing this book is to ask forgiveness of the people we are threatening. For far too long, I was willing to accept the possibility of not only my but their annihilation. Our security complex has made us believe that more and more weapons can bring peace and security. Our security complex makes us say, "We are really always against more and more weapons, but unfortunately the Communists are forcing us to continue the arms race." Our security complex offers us a bogus justification for planning mass murder, suicide, and the annihilation of all life. This complex afflicts not only politicians, but everyone who lets politicians continue the arms race. *We are planning suicide because we are afraid of peace.* We are so irrationally fixated on the outer enemy—the enemy *around* us—that we are unable to recognize the inner enemy, the enemy *inside* us. Yet the prerequisite of peace around us is peace inside us. "Judge not, that you be not judged," says Jesus. Our moral arrogance toward Communists blocks our realistic view of our own nuclear sins. In the Atomic Age, Christians, who claim to be lovers of peace, are confronted with the alternative: faith in God or faith in the bomb? If you believe in the God of Jesus, in the God of love, then you cannot believe in the bomb. Our faith in the bomb as a guarantee of security grew as our faith in God vanished.

The Good Samaritan is called "blessed" by Jesus not because

he helped an injured man, but because he was merciful to his enemy. Atomic armaments are collective mercilessness, collective hatred of the enemy. The nuclear arms race is an utterance of our sick souls. Why should this diagnosis apply only to Eastern Europe? In December 1982, Helmut Kohl said that the Soviets have to understand that more and more weapons cannot bring peace. It would, of course, be nice if the Soviets understood this. But why in the name of all that's holy should the Soviets be the only ones to understand it? Who is keeping up the arms race at present? Don't the politicians realize what they are saying? The ideological labels—Christian or Communist—that the participants in the arms race have put on themselves say nothing. All that counts is what they do. Someone has to start by stopping. If not the East, then the West. If not the West, then the East. Starting to stop will be the "ultimate IQ test of mankind" (Heinz Haber). If we don't pass this test, then there will be no more tests to pass.

Bishop Krusche told us that he was criticized by the local leaders of the Socialist Unity Party because four adolescents who had taken part in a silent march for peace had carried burning candles and a sign: DON'T LET IT HAPPEN AGAIN! Later, in the car, Norbert Blüm said to me, "Our system is better, we can do things like that." Of course we can. Bishop Krusche's experience does not exactly show the superiority of present-day socialism; it exposes its weakness and anxieties. It reveals how difficult it is to live peacefully with a government that is scared of four burning candles or a little bit of cardboard that says, SWORDS INTO PLOWSHARES. It is certainly difficult to achieve a nuclear freeze with political leaders who are being eaten up by their security complex; nevertheless, we have to do it.

Western countries also come down hard on peaceniks. Just think of the many stupid and uninformed remarks by high-ranking government officials. In the West, these attacks are more subtle and are often made under a veil of tolerance.

When West Germany's Christian Democratic Union mounted a peace demonstration on June 5, 1982, in Bonn, I had my cameraman film a group from the Young People's Union, which also took part in the peace demonstration sponsored by the peace movement five days later. Members of the Young People's Union carried the same signs at both events: NO WEAPONS FOR THE THIRD WORLD, PEACE BEGINS WITHIN US, SWORDS INTO PLOWSHARES, and WEAPONS DON'T FILL YOUR STOMACH. At both demonstrations, the first thing these young people heard was: "You're at the wrong demonstration." No filmmaker could have devised a better scenario. At the CDU demonstration, they were told, "You've come five days too early." At the peace-movement event, they were told, "You've come five days too late." And at the first demonstration, their signs were actually pulled down by participants for whom the only valid peace slogans were those favoring the NATO double resolution. When I was filming the scene, I was yelled at: "Commie infiltrator! . . . Go to East German TV! . . ." The Young People's Union members pointed out that they belonged to the Christian Democratic party. "Don't get snotty!" they were told. The fear of peace runs deep.

Citing the Sermon on the Mount can trigger violent reactions. What would have happened to Jesus had he gone to a demonstration of a Christian party and spoken in the spirit of the Sermon? If a West European is scared of peace demonstrators, and if an East European is scared of the words *swords into plowshares,* how much more frightened are they of real peace? The main obstacle to peace is the inability of most people to imagine peace between the East and the West.

Many politicians try to inspire fear in their opponents by means of the nuclear arms buildup because they themselves are scared of peace. Or do they merely lack imagination? The following question might help us to achieve peace: If the opponent is as scared of me as I am of him, how can I help him get over his fear?

Our chief problem can no longer be: How can I protect myself against my enemy? The most important issue now is: How can I protect my enemy against myself? This would be intelligent love of the enemy. We can get closer to peace only by ridding ourselves of our moral arrogance. We must understand that our current political ethics is a holier-than-thou attitude. We have merely been pointing our finger at the other person's wicked ways and failed to see our own.

The Christian Democratic Union in the East and the Christian Democratic Union in the West

Six weeks after my conversations in East Germany, the East German CDU held a convention in Dresden. This East German city is the German Hiroshima. It was almost totally destroyed in 1945. And here, in the autumn of 1982, Gerald Götting, the head of the East German CDU, was defending "his" atomic bombs: Friendship with the Soviet Union is the foundation of our state; the (East German) CDU is fighting against the NATO arms buildup; the East and the West should not be placed on the same level in arms talks. The only danger comes from Western imperialism; the only thing coming from the East is peace.

If we interchange the words *East* and *West* in his speech, then we have the kind of speech that my party colleagues give in West Germany: The danger comes from the East; the foundation of our politics is our friendship with the United States; the West German CDU is fighting against the Soviet arms buildup. . . .

Erich Honecker said, "The [East German] army is a peace movement." And, as we drove back, Norbert Blüm said to me, "The East German CDU is totally dependent on Moscow." I think so too. The East German CDU is probably more dependent on Moscow than the West German CDU is on Washington.

Many pronuclear arguments used by official politicians in

East and West Germany are interchangeable. Bonn and East Berlin are both interested in the success of arms talks. But neither government is willing to admit the lethal outcome of a further arms race if the SALT talks or equivalent talks are not resumed. For both German governments, allegiance to allies has absolute priority. Similarly, in the face of economic difficulties and increasing national debts, neither German state will seriously discuss any reduction of its military budget. The organized lack of peace is still cultivated to the detriment of real security by way of disarmament. Is it truly in our national interest to keep giving in to the notions of the nuclear superpowers? In the 1980's, the danger for both German states is neither "communism" nor "capitalism." Both countries are threatened by atomic bombs, which both the East and the West have built out of ignorance of one another and fear of one another. And they will keep building them until we stop them. Nuclear weapons are not an item in "capitalist" or "communist" politics. They cannot be fought with the class-struggle theory by the Right or the Left. The struggle against atomic death is not a fight to save a class. It is a fight to save humanity.

In November 1982, after a conversation with General Bernard Rogers, the American commander-in-chief of NATO, Chancellor Kohl and Defense Minister Wörner declared that they were in "complete agreement with the United States in regard to NATO strategy." A short time earlier, Rogers had told journalists in Hamburg, "Since we still have some catching-up to do in the conventional area, we would have to use atomic weapons quickly in case of a conflict." It's not hard to imagine in which country these nuclear weapons would be used first. Could it ever be in Germany's interest to become the nuclear battlefield of the superpowers?

Anyone who is serious about reunifying Germany (in whatever form) has to support everything that promotes the emancipation of either German state from its respective superpower. This emancipatory process (which is not directed against anyone) could begin, quite sensibly, with the armaments issue. Only a liberation of the two states as atomic hostages of the superpowers will put the German question back on the agenda of history. The arms race makes it difficult to pursue a reunification policy and a peace policy in Europe. Konrad Adenauer said as much in a speech on August 14, 1961:

> Please recall Stalin's motives for placing all these satellite states in front of Soviet Russia: Yugoslavia, Bulgaria, Rumania, Hungary, Poland, Czechoslovakia, and the GDR [East Germany]. He was afraid that Russia would some day be attacked by the West, so he wanted to make sure that the decisive battles in such a war would be fought inside these countries and not in Soviet Russia. Remember that in those days Soviet Russia did not yet have nuclear armaments, which, after all, have altered the whole picture—have totally changed the whole picture of any possible future war. Once a *controlled disarmament* allows these countries to stop fulfilling the purpose that Stalin gave them, then—I am firmly convinced—the time will have come when our country, Germany, will be released from its division and become a great, united Germany.

As far back as the early 1960's, Adenauer was advocating the realistic thesis that today's military doctrines prevent peace in Central Europe as well as the reunification of Germany. There can be no German reunification without a nonnuclear Europe.

Abuse of the Sermon on the Mount

In 1975, a "Catholic catechism" appeared in Switzerland. It says, "Are the instructions in the Sermon on the Mount to be taken literally? The instructions in the Sermon on the Mount are not to be taken literally, because that would create unendurable conditions in both private and public life." Here, in a "Catholic catechism," Jesus is declared a fool—in the name of Christianity.

In politics as in our private lives, we are often on the level of "an eye for an eye, a tooth for a tooth." This is generally the level of our so-called Christian ethics today.

The idea of relativity has remained valid even in our present-day jurisprudence. Jesus, however, smashed through this law of regulated retaliation. He wanted something radically new. Two thousand years ago, his thinking was more progressive than ours today: not revenge, but love, even love of one's enemies. Franz Kamphaus, the bishop of Limburg, West Germany, said something about this at the 1982 Catholic convention in Düsseldorf: "What can I do to turn the opponent [enemy] . . . into a partner in peace? After all, I can't remain indifferent to him. God loves him just as He loves me." If one agrees with this interpretation of the Sermon on the Mount, can he keep aiming nuclear rockets at his enemies?

In the summer of 1982, President Reagan took part in a military game at the Pentagon. They were rehearsing a nuclear World War III. Reagan's subsequent statement to journalists was revealing: "I pray that I never have to launch these terrible atomic weapons." His distress was probably genuine. After all, he had just participated in the run-through of an "atomic scenario" for killing millions upon millions of people. Yet such distress remains futile if the arms race goes on. The expression of distress is no substitute for a nuclear freeze and no real proof of an ability to make peace. For Jesus, any religion that stands only for pious formulas and a literal interpretation of the law is not sufficiently moved by the Spirit: "Every one who hears these words of mine and does not do them will be like a foolish man who built his house upon the sand." One can abuse the Sermon on the Mount in an election campaign. And one can also abuse it by not taking it seriously or by ignoring it.

For anyone who wishes to follow Jesus, the Sermon on the Mount leaves no room to doubt its validity. It demands deeds from Christians, not words; it demands an emulation of Christ, not a heedless imitation. The sheer veneration of Christ often makes us put him, as a model, on a pedestal or project him beyond the clouds. Jesus becomes an object of Sunday worship but has no meaning for everyday life, for a Christian's work and politics. If a man prays that he will "never have to launch . . . terrible atomic weapons," he is ultimately passing the buck to God, giving Him the responsibility for any use of weapons of annihilation. God as a scapegoat for the most horrible deed in human history—and with a religious trimming! Religion as opium! Religion as a veiling of crime! This is precisely the kind of "religion" that leads to christening an atomic submarine *Corpus Christi:* profaning God in the name of God.

The Sermon on the Mount should also inspire skepticism about what politicians say. In February 1981, the *Frankfurter Rundschau,* a West German magazine, reported on a convention in Ludwigshafen. There, a retired general had said that as an active Christian he could ethically justify an annihilatory nuclear strike against Warsaw Pact countries after they attacked first—even if this strike were purely retaliatory and millions of innocent people were to die. For freedom, he said, was the highest good. And he was sure that priests would go along with his conviction.

Many people cite Jesus, but fail to notice that they crucify him by supposedly imitating him. This is an un-Christian Christianity. If someone goes by Jesus, and not by some projection onto Jesus, he must conclude without any theological frills— without any ifs, ands, or buts—that an atomic war can never be ethically justified under any circumstances. An atomic war is un-Christian. This applies both to the first strike and to the retaliatory strike. The traditional justification for *producing* nuclear weapons (for instance, in the Heidelberg theses of German Evangelical Christians, 1959) was based on the idea that this could prevent war. There can be no ethical justification for *using* atomic weapons.

But ever since both Eastern and Western politicians and military men have been speculating about "limited atomic war," about "winnable atomic war," and about "nuclear first strike," the old justification for producing atomic weapons is no longer valid. Now that the unthinkable has become thinkable, the production of offensive mass-annihilation weapons is a temptation of God. I cannot pray: Lord, give us the peace of nuclear equilibrium. Praying in order to spirit away the danger of nuclear war and simultaneously taking on the responsibility for more and more numerous, more and more ominous mass-murder weapons has a lot to do with raising spirits and nothing to do with Jesus of Nazareth. A person who moralizes cannot act morally. If worship and emulation are confused, then religion becomes a "superproduction" (Hanna Wolff), a protective shield, behind which one can do anything. This "religion" lulls the conscience rather than impelling it. If this goes on, nothing will change. "Faith" is no substitute for correct, responsible actions. A sentimental faith that promotes irresponsible behavior and prevents responsible behavior is a modern and, of course, unconscious crucifixion.

Carola Stern, a West German reporter, discovered the following inscription on the headstone of Julius Rupps, an 1848 German democrat: "Anyone who does not live in accordance with the truth that he professes is the most dangerous enemy of truth."

The truth of the Sermon on the Mount is not just truth, it is life. Jesus said, "I am the way, the truth, and the life." For Jesus, the worst people are those who pretend: he calls them hypocrites, adders, a nest of vipers. Christians who do not try to live in accordance with Jesus' central demand—to love one's enemies—are the greatest enemies of the Sermon on the Mount.

Who practices love of his enemies consistently? Who can throw the first stone here? Nearly all people are spiritually torn; they are made up of both good and evil; they want peace, but they often create dissension. Our only chance is to realize that we are torn and to stop projecting our own evil onto others; instead, we ought to work modestly on overcoming it. Being human means becoming human. An awareness of sin is the prerequisite for turning over a new leaf. Jesus is unequivocal: "Not every one who says to me, 'Lord, Lord,' shall enter the kingdom of heaven, but he who does the will of my Father who is in heaven."

History—including and especially the history of Christianity—is filled with examples of the greatest crimes with religious trimmings. Religion has been used as a coverup by Hitler and Khomeini, Khaddafi and Pinochet, Begin and Arafat.

C. G. Jung said, "Christ can be imitated to the point of stigmatization without the imitator even approximately imitating the model and his meaning." Perhaps that is the tragedy of the Christian religions—at least, in the industrial countries. They no longer reach the souls of most people. At best, they create illusions of a believed faith, a sentimentalized love, a pseudopeace. The outcome is a politics of a pathologically good conscience with no awareness of social sinning. Religion has a new name in the industrial countries: economics. If only the person who makes lots of money is considered successful, if economic growth is worshiped as a religion, if commodities replace truth, then neither true religion nor the true God has a place here. The word *soul* never crops up even once in all the 109 pages of the papal encyclical *Laborem Exercens*. And yet an encyclical is a guide written by the caretaker of souls in the largest Christian church. If the soul is forgotten, then religion has no chance; it degenerates into the red tape of formulas, which Jesus warned against.

The soul plays such a shadowy part in "enlightened" Christianity that one can expect little evil and certainly no good from it. Yet we can perceive the beauty of the sun only with our eyes, and we can experience God only with our souls. In a statement on World Peace Day, January 1, 1982, Pope John Paul II actually said that the psychological discoveries of our time were important for the investigation of peace. If we seriously view man as created in the image of God, then we know about the soul's relationship with God and we try to live—i.e. act—accordingly. Building atomic assault weapons is modern paganism, even if responsible politicians, scientists, and military men zealously claim to be Christians.

The production of nuclear arms and the threat to use them are, for Christians, at best an expression of a "believed faith," but not the expression of a "lived faith" (Johann Baptist Metz).

If a man advocates nuclear weapons today, then his soul is untouched by the spirit of Christ; a dark paganism rules his mind. A believed faith existed in Germany even during the Nazi period. The churches were full, but the hearts of the faithful were barely able to withstand. Most German Christians believed "with their backs to Auschwitz," as Metz put it. The American Bishop Hunthausen sees today's nuclear politics as the "Auschwitz of our time." After 1945, when their children asked about Auschwitz, many Germans said, "We didn't know anything about it." The point isn't whether or not they were telling the truth; there is no question that we cannot offer this answer to future generations—even if someone were left to ask. Anyone who wants to know knows.

Nuclear weapons are the most dreadful evidence of a pagan culture and a politics without a soul. "The Christian mission preaches the Gospel to poor, naked heathens; but the inner heathens that populate Europe are untouched by Christianity" (C. G. Jung). Anyone who does not personally experience the reality of the soul may be a learned theologian or a distinguished prince of the church or a popular politician. But he doesn't have the foggiest notion of religion. He is blind to the sun; he is inwardly inept and does not see the wickedness within him. And that is why, in his private life, at work, and in politics, he always needs scapegoats. However, the Sermon on the Mount is about life, not faith. Even two millennia after people first heard its tidings, the Sermon has still not reached our politics, our society, or, to any extent, our private lives. It was not a program for a bygone era. Are we mentally ready today, are our souls ripe for the nonviolence of the Sermon on the Mount?

THREE

The New Politics

*Today we are continually being astounded at the discoveries
made in the area of violence. I can guarantee that far more
astonishing and seemingly impossible discoveries can be made
in the area of nonviolence.*
—Mahatma Gandhi

Are We Ripe for the Sermon on the Mount?

Do we have the strength to repent and to free ourselves?

We have to learn that our goal in the industrial countries should be a weaning away from materialism, rather than more and more pampering, if the tensions between the Northern and the Southern hemispheres are not to lead to further wars. We can preserve creation only if we realize that the atomic bomb is the zenith of our one-sided materialism. The issue today is not liberation from powerlessness, but liberation from military and economic superiority. The world will hardly become more human with today's destructive, macho, revolutionary values; it *can* become more human with the life-preserving, female, evolutionary virtues. It's no picnic living in accordance with the Sermon on the Mount, but no one who would like to be a Christian can free himself from its aims. My impression is that men have a harder time dealing with the Sermon than women do. Women know more about love.

We will be ripe for the Sermon on the Mount once we realize that the all-important question in our current situation is: Life or death? We have to understand that militarized thinking and the bubbly and optimistic trivialization of the looming nuclear holocaust are as dangerous as the bomb itself.

We will be ripe for the Sermon on the Mount once we understand what the preacher is saying: Things can't go on this way. More and more weapons, more and more environmental destruction, more and more starvation, more and more spiritual crippling—the earth cannot endure it. Of course, the Sermon is no patented recipe. But it does outline a stance: We have to be as concerned about other people's lives as we are about our own. So far, all revolutions have proved that one cannot "create" a "new man." Yet Jesus wants the new human being, the new heaven, and the new earth. However, *this* new human being can come only from within us. The failure of all socialist revolutions is due to the socialist belief that human beings can be changed if conditions or the outer, material human being is changed— naturally under pressure and coercion. The results are well known. Human beings cannot *be* changed, *human beings can only change themselves.* Jesus wants a repentance of the heart, a spiritual revolution, a faith that can move mountains.

The goal of this repentance is not the *homo oeconomicus,* the economic man, but the *homo humanus,* the whole human being. The goal is a human revolution with political consequences. We can change ourselves if we want to change ourselves. All true change begins within ourselves. The message of the Sermon on the Mount is: "You are blessed if *you* . . ." People object, saying that not even the most pious can live in peace if the evil neighbor doesn't want to. But this sidesteps the problem in two ways.

First of all, this objection presumes that we ourselves (the West) are good, and the other (the East) is bad. Thus, we lack all knowledge of ourselves.

Second, we are once again demanding from the other something that we are not willing to practice ourselves: nonviolence.

"So long as the Communists do not make the Sermon on the Mount the foundation of their politics, we cannot do so either." I keep hearing this statement, especially in Christian circles. People need scapegoats if they don't live as they ought to in terms of what is considered respectable Christianity. People need the image of the enemy, saying, Do unto others before they do unto you. However, Christ did not let himself be nailed to the cross for the sake of that cynical old rule. The Sermon on the Mount is neither a sentimental romance nor an aesthetic radicalism. It is not a commandment, it is *the* offer of a humane life. The insight gleaned from the Sermon is: Only love helps; hatred makes us worse.

Threatening the other with an arms buildup is not helpful to him or to me. My escalation forces him into a further buildup, and his forces me to go on in the same way. The Golden Rule is: "Do unto others as you would have them do unto you." So if I don't want the other person to continue his arms buildup, then I shouldn't continue mine, even if he keeps on with his. We not only have to protect our enemies against us, we also and primarily have to protect ourselves against ourselves. The Christian virtues of faith, hope, love, patience, and humility apply not only to our behavior toward others, but to our behavior toward ourselves. Charity begins at home. Peace begins within us. There is no other way of understanding the Old Testament commandment: "You shall love your neighbor as yourself." I myself am dependent on my own love because evil is within me. According to an old story, Adam, the first man, recognized his other side, evil, when he saw himself in a mirror. He now lost his "heavenly innocence"; he became "knowing." Today, the man who threatens to use atomic bombs in seeming innocence does not know what he is doing; he knows nothing about his other side. This other side, the evil within us, is not made harmless by our failure to admit it. Quite the contrary: it is extremely dangerous, precisely because it exists without our admitting it. Psychologists tell us that we project our evil onto others only because we repress it and fail to discern our "shadow." If you ignore your own enemy within you, then you will need the image of an enemy. If you seek evil everywhere, but not in yourself, then you will ultimately build atomic bombs while condemning others for doing likewise, and sooner or later you will use your bombs. You will regard your own nuclear mentality as legitimate, for evil must be fought. The less you recognize the evil within you, the more intensely you fight it in others. A man can threaten to use atomic bombs only if he does not realize that he is threatening himself.

We fail to recognize the link between the politics of the bomb and the destruction of our souls because we do not know ourselves. Self-knowledge is always the first step in the right direction. It is the prerequisite for self-education. Meditating on the Sermon on the Mount is a way of gaining self-knowledge. Saint Augustine said about self-knowledge: "What good is it if we so carefully examine and properly grasp the essence of all things and yet fail to know ourselves?" The goal of all self-knowledge is "the divine core in the human heart" (Jolande Jacobi). Since the soul is of a divine nature, this goal remains—almost—unattainable on earth, but we still ought to strive for it. The God of Jesus of Nazareth is a God of love; thus, He is patient and indulgent toward moral imperfection and wickedness. Threatening with the bomb means threatening one's own soul. Right after the first atomic bombs were used in 1945, Pierre Teilhard de Chardin wrote about humanity: "Its body was whole. But what had happened to its soul?" The atomic bomb had turned man "into a new being that did not know itself." Now man revels "in a feeling of infinitely developed power." He has "bitten into the fruit of the great discovery" and has had "a taste of supercreation."

The more nuclear bombs come into the foreground, the more the soul is pushed into the background. The logical consequence is the inner, spiritual illnesses afflicting more and more people. Have there ever been so many neurotics, so many drug addicts, so many suicidal individuals, so many people incapable of a relationship, so many socially motivated abortions, so much inner emptiness, so little basic trust as in our time? The bomb has already wrought spiritual havoc. Our psyches all suffer from nuclear contamination. Even worse, we don't realize it. And worst of all, most politicians don't want to realize it. If our souls die altogether, then all that will remain is the end of the world.

Is there a more humane humanism than God's humanism if God (according to Saint John) "is love"? The God of the preacher of the Sermon on the Mount is a God of love. A God of love is a passionately humane God.

The real peace utopia of the Sermon on the Mount is not the dream image of an unreal world; it is the design and the knowledge—or at least the first draft and the foreknowledge—of a world that should and can be different. Today, the real utopia of the Sermon reveals not only the goal of peace, but also the way to peace: no further arms buildup, no further steps in the old direction, but at least a nuclear freeze as the first step in the right direction. The law of peace stated in the Sermon goes: Peace exists not against the other, but only with him. Peace can exist only if one person takes the first step, unconditionally. "A peace politics is a politics of the first step," said Werner Krusche, bishop of Magdeburg, in 1971. Today this means: In order to end the arms race, someone must start to stop, *unconditionally.* So, no further arms buildup! A basic law of psychology tells us that if you want to get someone to do something, you first have to do it yourself. If you want to get the Soviet Union to disarm, you first have to stop your arms buildup. There is no other way. We know this not only from the Sermon on the Mount, psychology, and common sense (how common is it?), but also from our dismal experiences with all the arms talks. This simple truth is not only unrecognized today, but jeered at. For centuries, the motto was: If you want peace, prepare for war. Today, in the Atomic Era, the only motto can be: If you want peace, prepare for peace. This means: If you want disarmament, you have to disarm. The road decides the goal. The end does not justify the means; at most, bad means have always rendered the best ends unjust. Gandhi's philosophy of peace: "Unclean means have unclean results."

"One cannot reach the truth by means of untruth." Everything has its consequences. Long before the war breaks out, it is prepared; that is, it has already begun in people's minds and in the media. Today, there are not too few, but too many weapons. And West Germany is the country with the greatest density of nuclear arms.

Anyone in Western Europe who wants more rockets, weapons, and bombs will reap what he has sown. He will be an accomplice. The fact that the other side is also a sinner and an accomplice can never justify one's own sin and guilt. Violence is merely followed by even greater violence, not by salvation. The world can still be saved through Gandhi's nonviolence and the love of Jesus of Nazareth. All politicians, all who are pro- or antinuclear, assure us that of course they want peace. Nor can any rational person doubt it. Yet the desires of the politicians have no more political effect than the yearnings of the peace movement. Deeds are what count, not words. The fact that—nearly—all politicians want peace is obvious; but the means they use to attain this goal reveal their true colors. The arms systems discussed in today's arms talks are annihilatory, not defensive. Only the right means allow us to achieve the right goals. We can reach life only by taking the right ways. The leitmotif of foreign politics in the West has always been: How can we prevent the Soviet Union from attacking us? By now at the latest, when the danger of all-out annihilation keeps growing, the new and sensible motif of our foreign politics should be: How can we get the Soviet Union interested in dismantling its destruction potential? So long as the negotiations follow Lenin's thesis that "Trust is good; control is better," there can be no progress. Someone must start to stop. We have to turn Lenin's maxim upside down: Control is good; trust is better. But why does the West try to out-Lenin the Soviet Union at arms talks? This policy is foolish, if only because the economic plight of Eastern

Europe demands disarmament more than the economic problems of Western countries. All our experience tells us that a nuclear freeze would be more useful than an arms buildup. We would be more ripe for the Sermon on the Mount.

A Peace Council of All Religions

Gandhi said, "I can say without the least hesitation that the man who claims that religion has nothing to do with politics does not know the meaning of religion." Peace needs a lobby. The great religions need to form a worldwide coalition and become the peace lobby. A peace council, made up of the leaders of the great religions, could give real impetus to more pressure on and resistance to the current nuclear politics. The goal of such a council: All religious people on earth would be asked to boycott any war measures and any production of mass-annihilation weapons.

In November 1982, I met the Dalai Lama. He spoke to me of peace ethics from a Buddhist point of view, which is another version of the peace ethics of the Sermon on the Mount. All religions are flowers from the same garden; they grow from the same humus. The Dalai Lama told me, "Love is stronger than hate." In November 1982, in Madrid, the pope told a group of scientists, "It is a scandal of our era that many scientists devote themselves to perfecting new war weapons that could someday prove lethal." Does such a speech have political consequences? Today, some 30 million people, including 400,000 scientists, are working in the armaments industry. I would guess that most of these workers were baptized as Christians. So far, their consciences have not been reached by the church. The fault lies primarily with the church, whose very leaders have not developed a true spirit of resistance to nuclear sins. Theologians often let truth go begging. They have truth in their minds, but they do not reach the heart because they do not really seek reality.

People today are not asking about achieved truths; they are looking for ways that lead to truth. Paul Tillich said, "Truth is dead without the road to truth." The search for truth is more important than dogmas about truth. The sharpest critic of Christianity as it exists is Jesus himself. Jesus did not found a religion; he wanted people to find a religious life.

The Central Committee of [West] German Catholics has approved the arms buildup. If the pope feels it is a sin to take part in the production of mass-annihilation weapons, then it is certainly a sin to deploy these weapons. If the West German bishops took the pope's statement seriously, they would have to take a clear-cut position against any further arms escalation. John Paul II has said, "The nuclear arms race will lead to war." The pope's fine words have failed to inspire any deeds on the part of the Catholic Church in West Germany. As Helmut Gollwitzer put it, this is a "great tragedy." Heinrich Böll wryly asks, "Is German Catholicism in its corporateness a NATO Catholicism?"

In the United States, "Catholic" means to be *against* the buildup. In West Germany, it means to be *for* it. Many German Catholics need their image of the enemy, so that their image of the world may look right. Jesus wanted to liberate us from this. As early as the 1950's, Reinhold Schneider felt that *the* mortal sin of the churches was that they could not say no to nuclear weapons. He called this attitude a "rejection of the Gospel."

The Catholic Church of West Germany has been at the forefront of the fight for unborn life. *Pro vita:* the right to life must also involve a concern for those already born and for future generations. Joining the struggle against nuclear death is also a question of credibility and identity for the Catholic Church. There is life after birth and life before death. Jesus always spoke of the conditions for *this* life. Jesus was political. For too long a time, the stance of West Germany's Catholic Church in regard to the peace issue has been a betrayal of the man of peace from

Nazareth. Today, we can see the coming death of the world. Some churches have woken up: the Catholic Church in the United States, Holland, and Italy; the Protestant Church in East Germany; the Anglican Church in England. Catholic bishops are at the head of the North American peace movement. The East German peace movement would be inconceivable without the Protestant Church. Its majority is moving toward a political pacifism. Church peace initiatives have inspired several politicians to change their minds. Kurt Biedenkopf wrote in *Report:* "We have taken the wrong road, reached the nuclear peak, and are now at the edge of the abyss. We have to go back." Richard von Weizsäcker said, "The peace movement is a healthy thing for politics." The wind can shift with the help of the churches. Without the resistance of the various confessions, there can be no peace. The leadership committee of the Catholic Church Council in the United States has this to say about Washington's policies:

> Previously, there was a growing willingness to see the world in its true variety and differences. . . . In contrast to this, the government is now determined to make America number one in the world. Not number one in literature, life expectancy, or aid to less-developed countries; not number one in freedom from infant mortality, drug consumption, criminality, and suicide; but rather, number one in military superiority, the ability to force our will or kill countless human beings in the attempt.

On October 1, 1982, at the end of the Franciscan Year, the heads of the four Franciscan orders wrote, "Both the use of atomic weapons and the nuclear-arms race must be judged as immoral."

At least *one* Catholic bishop in England thought about the Sermon on the Mount during the Falklands War: Bishop Guazelli, chairman of the British Pax Christi movement, condemned the government's use of violence in front of an audience of 600 young people. The pacifist bishop was then asked by an agitated TV reporter, "Are you trying to tell us that we should turn the other cheek in such international conflicts?" The bishop replied, "Yes, perhaps we should. Given the nuclear weapons and the international involvements, I really believe that someday we will reach a point at which common sense will dictate that we turn the other cheek; for if someone doesn't turn the other cheek, then sooner or later there will be no cheeks to turn."

Still another man dared to go by Jesus' words. Would it really have been a defeat for Prime Minister Margaret Thatcher if she had gone along with the U.N. mediation efforts, so that several hundred young Britons and Argentinians might still be alive today? Once again, young people who did not know one another had to kill each other on behalf of politicians who knew one another very well! A military solution for the Falkland Islands is no solution at all in political terms. Whenever someone has been defeated, the seed has already been planted for the next war. If the pope and the Dalai Lama, the patriarch of Constantinople and the World Council of Churches jointly asked their followers to refrain from taking any further financial or physical part in war preparations, then that would be a loud and clear signal for peace, a worldwide politics of peace.

It is the job of religions to call a spade a spade, to tell the truth. But the churches do not ask too much of their members; they ask almost nothing of them. There is nothing more boring than boring churches. Christ's church exists for the sake of peace, not the other way around! If, despite their moral investment in peace, which they all prize, the great religions do not take a more concrete, practical, and political part in the struggle for peace, then they will be guilty of failing to provide moral support.

It is not socialism that spells danger for religion today, but rather religion's lack of imagination, its lack of a sense of utopia.

The prophets in the churches must get together with the wise men in science to encourage the visionaries in politics. If, first, all religions join forces in a peace council, put up a united front against legalizing nuclear mass murder, and strengthen their followers' sense of sin, then peace will finally have a lobby.

Love Your Enemies!

Jesus' love of enemies is the core of the Sermon on the Mount. In connection with the preceding text on retaliation, it is clear that no other statement that has come down from him is as radical and hard-line. The love of enemies is also linked to the suggestion that we be modest: "Judge not, that you be not judged." Jesus' appeal is meant for all those who flaunt their clean records. Don't appoint yourselves judges! Get rid of your prejudices! Auschwitz and Dachau, Treblinka and Sobibor were possible only on a foundation of solid prejudice. What the Jews were back then, the Communists are today, or the foreigners. After 1945, Max Picard rightly pointed to the "Hitler within us." Let's not fool ourselves. "Judge not." That refers to all of us. We ourselves are capable of anything. Occasionally, our dreams may remind us of the evil within us. We are what we dream. Dreams come from our heart of hearts.

"Judge not" does not mean "Accept everything about the other person." It means "Try to understand him." "Don't be hypocrites." "Form a judgment, but do not condemn." For our present political topic, this means: Do not ask others to disarm if you are not going to disarm yourself. First do what you expect others to do. Set a good example. The Chinese philosopher Lao-tsu called this virtue "teaching without words." It is the first principle of all upbringing that is based on love and not punishment. If you set a good example for your children, you can spare your words.

Our moral arrogance toward people who think differently is certainly one of the fundamental reasons for the lack of peace in our world. Today, loving our enemies means that Communists are our brothers and sisters because *all* human beings have the same father. Often, however, our interiorized anticommunism is a kind of substitute religion.

Martin Buber offers a simple reason for brotherly love: "Love your neighbor; he is like you." Unless we love ourselves, we will be incapable of loving our enemies or our neighbors. If you are at odds with yourself, if you are inwardly torn, if you cannot develop love for your true self, you will always be a burden on others. There is no more sensible reason to love your enemy than to say, Love your enemy; he is like you.

Loving one's enemies is not an attempt to rid the world of conflict and aggression. However, it is an attempt to struggle without bloodshed or threats. Love of enemies does not mean glossing over conflicts; it means bridging them so that opponents can come together. Finding a civilized way of struggling is not only a political task but a religious task. Love of enemies means projecting yourself into the other person's situation and security concerns: If I keep up the arms race, what will I provoke the other to do? How can I get him to *stop* the arms race?

Politicians should not remain under the pressure of the military and the armaments industry. They should stop saying that a continual arms buildup will increase a country's security by increasing the risk for the opponent. Today, love of enemies has become the logic of survival.

Theologians all agree that love of enemies and nonviolence are authentic goals of Jesus. "You have heard that it was said, 'You shall love your neighbor and hate your enemy.' But I say unto you, Love your enemies" (Matthew 5:43).

Jesus' new tidings are an onslaught on the old society; they demand a new social behavior. A new social behavior on the part of the individual creates new conditions in the society. This new demand is meant to correct what "scribes and Pharisees" had considered just. Matthew ends the passage about love of enemies with a surprising statement: "You, therefore, must be perfect, as your heavenly Father is perfect." This is a revolution in the history of religion. The meaning here is not ascetic perfection, but a wholeness and haleness in the Hebrew sense: the verb *shalom* means "to make whole, sound, complete." One might also speak of "intactness," "good health." Man's wholeness should correspond to God's wholeness. Here we have Jesus' new image of God and his new image of man. Almost none of us has ever encountered *this* God and *this* human being in our religious instruction. Love of enemies seems so incomprehensibly alien because our Sunday-school teachers gave us an image of the judging God and not the loving God. Understanding love of enemies means understanding Jesus' image of God and of man.

In current political debate, we find the fiercest resistance to loving enemies. I can understand this resistance if only because that was what I was saying and writing just a few years ago: That's not part of politics; that's daydreaming, that's naive, that's pure utopia. Since then, I have come to realize that I did not understand Jesus. If you put down love of enemies as a crackpot notion, you should at least be honest with yourself and admit that you are calling Jesus a crackpot.

The central verse in Luke is: "Be merciful, even as your Father is merciful." Josef Blank says, "Here, the love of enemies becomes a participation in the saving, salvation-bringing love of God Himself, an evidence of His working of salvation in the world." Jesus even suggests that we pray for our enemies. Every honest prayer is at least an interruption of violence.

Love of enemies and nonviolence are linked. For Jesus, the violent man is inwardly the loser; he is unfree. If the man who is inwardly free and inwardly superior does not make a generous start in a conflict, then there is no escape from this vicious circle of violence and counterviolence. Love of enemies is not moronic; it is intelligent. Love of enemies means having the courage to take the first step. It is mental sovereignty instead of anxious calculation and selfish insistence on being right. Love of enemies is not theological small change that can be traded off; it is the will of the Creator.

Jesus' love of enemies is not a commandment and not a law. Freedom, not coercion, is *the* essential characteristic of Jesus. One cannot imitate Jesus slavishly, but one can try to live in his spirit. This emulation is possible only if we make Jesus' demands first upon ourselves, both privately and politically.

What Should We Do?

If we know what has already been prepared and what is now being prepared in the nuclear world, then we cannot and must not just stand there and do nothing. We will not prevent nuclear suicide by shrugging our shoulders and maintaining a blind confidence in politics or fatalism. We can no longer say, It's none of my business.

So far, mankind has put up with the atomic threat as something fateful and unavoidable. The official policies have labeled the fight against atomic death "extreme" and "utopian," and their own armaments madness "realistic" and "correct." What's "realistic" is that the governments of the world spend as much on armaments in 2 days as the United Nations spends in 365 days in its struggle against hunger and disease. What's "extreme" is regarding this reality as insane and trying to change it. Neither the human soul nor the earth can endure this condition much longer. If mankind does not wake up and fight against its cowardly rationalizations, then nuclear death will win. We must first understand that the dreamers claim they are pursuing a realistic policy and accuse the realists of being "dreamers."

True rationality today lies in a convinced and convincing NO to any further arms buildup and arms race. We Germans must remind Helmut Kohl of *this* part of his state-of-the-nation address, if he continues the arms buildup: "To create peace with *fewer and fewer* weapons: This is the mission of our time." Remind the advocates of the arms buildup of their duty to make peace—remind them in letters and meetings! Influence public opinion by writing to newspapers and talking to journalists. Join the political parties. Get involved in the peace movement and start peace groups everywhere. We are not powerless.

Conservatives ought to be in the vanguard of this struggle, for we have to conserve the most precious thing we have: life. If the vicious circle of an eternal arms race is not broken, then soon there will be nothing left to conserve. The wish to have the world as it used to be is not the only thing that can be called conservative. Today, conservatives worthy of the name must fight to preserve creation. Conservatives must become aware of their skepticism toward progress in regard to weapons of annihilation. Conservatives and Christians ought to be immune to nuclear pressure. Yet why do Christians of all people fall prey to Karl Marx's erroneous theory that "being molds our consciousness"? Why won't Christians give in to Jesus' teaching: Change being with your consciousness. Friedrich Nietzsche called Jesus' love of enemies decadent. Today, many conservatives and many Christians have sided with Nietzsche rather than with Jesus.

We must not leave the world to the technocratic gamblers, who see no prospect of meaning in their lives and actions and have therefore become nihilists. We have to free the nihilists from their nihilism by not letting ourselves catch their germ.

Repentance is not child's play. The groups closest to the weapons have the hardest time with repentance: generals, politicians, scientists. Generals often have little faith in a peaceful world. Scientists are often imprisoned in an ivory tower, and politicians are too dependent on their parties. It was obviously easier for them to dig our grave than to fill it up again today.

Now that the professional politicians have led us to the brink of disaster, we laymen have no choice but to sound a many-voiced retreat together. All people throughout the world who can talk, write, and organize must now talk, write, and work politically. We can still use the reprieve that we have been granted.

The goal of the struggle against nuclear arms is not to condemn the politicians, but to save the world. We are struggling *for* something. Politicians are not enemies in our struggle for peace; they are our partners in a conflict. Our goal must be to win them over as partners in peace. If anyone in the peace movement says that politicians are warmongers, he doesn't know what he's talking about and he is hurting the possibility of peace.

Will we become accomplices of death by sleeping and repressing, or will we become accomplices of life by acting? A prerequisite for a successful struggle for peace is the realization that our activities are useful only if we first achieve a certain understanding. I can think of no better training for this mental struggle than the Sermon on the Mount. Lev Kopelev, who, as a Russian soldier, practiced love of enemies toward German soldiers, is convinced that "the Sermon on the Mount is the highest, purest peak that the human spirit can achieve. The peace tidings of the Sermon on the Mount, which preaches love even of hate-filled enemies, was first heard by a tiny audience, a few hundred shepherds, fishermen, farmers, and pious students; by the poor, suffering, humiliated, defenseless people in a very tiny country." Since then, the Sermon has often been drowned out by the war din of the last 2,000 years. And yet it has survived.

This basic law of love and nonviolence still inspires those who seek peace with a vocabulary, strength, and imagination. The nonviolence of the preacher demands endurance. Jesus said, "By your endurance you will gain your lives" (Luke 21:19).

Luckily, Jesus was no theoretician; he was a practical man. His teaching was: Just start—nothing will work without you. That is, you have to act as if peace depended on you alone. Human beings decided to build atomic bombs, and human beings can agree to get rid of them. In the struggle for peace, our emotionalism, which "realists" call a weakness, can be our strength. The weakness of organized politics is its *lack* of emotionalism. Emotionally, one cannot be for, only against nuclear weapons. It is only in the joint struggle against atomic armaments of death that we can learn that we are not helpless. Everyone must learn that he has to be an expert, because peace is his business. The feeling of powerlessness and resignation is the true prerequisite for atomic annihilation. Resignation makes us passive; conscious work toward peace makes us active.

The question of what we can do is answered by the German novelist Günther Anders:

> Have no fear of fear, have the courage to fear. And have the courage to make others fear. Frighten your neighbor as yourself. Naturally, this kind of fear has to be something very special. (1) A fearless fear, since it excludes fear of those who might jeer at us for being scared. (2) An animating fear, since it ought to get us out of our corners and into the streets. (3) A loving fear, which should worry *about* the world, and not just about what might happen to us.

And the most important labor of peace: If we explain peace to our children, they will never declare war on others. But only a person who lives peace can explain peace to children.

First Steps: 1. Stop the Arms Buildup

Politics doesn't operate in such a way that West Germany could leave NATO overnight and disband its own army. The struggle against nuclear weapons has a fighting chance only if the peace movement realizes that politics is a step-by-step business. The crucial thing is for the peace movement to look for support among thoughtful people in all political camps. I can picture two specific steps that would not endanger the legitimate security interests of West Germany. Both steps could also be taken by conservative politicians. I know that some of the leading Christian Democratic politicians have thought about my thesis, "Someone has to start to stop; otherwise, the armaments madness will never stop." Thus, I am not suggesting a one-sided disarmament. My first goal is a one-sided nuclear freeze, something the majority of Americans would approve of. It would also have to be approved by the majority of West Germans. A nuclear freeze is the prerequisite for total disarmament. A reversal begins when we halt on the wrong path. Only then can we go toward disarmament step by step. If you wish to change our politics, you must figure out specific ways of changing it. Not everyone in the peace movement is doing this.

The Soviet Union is assuming that at this time an "approximate military equilibrium" exists between East and West. The West denies this and points to the SS-20's with which the Soviet Union is supposedly trying to get the upper hand. I can't tell which side is right. But I can imagine that if the West were to stop its arms buildup now, we would come closer to the goal of true disarmament than if the West stuck to the second part of the NATO double resolution. President Reagan's first step—turning SALT (arms limitation) into START (arms reduction)—would

probably be more promising. I can't be certain. But I am thinking of the atmosphere of future negotiations and the political
psychology involved. I am thinking that Kohl and Strauss keep
assuring us that the Soviet Union doesn't want war either. If all
this is true, then the gamble of an immediate halt to the arms
buildup would bring more rather than less security. I've used the
word *gamble*. Without such a gamble, I can see absolutely no way
of ending the arms race. Immediately after the start of arms
installation, the West could at least accept the minimal demand
of Pax Christi: stop the arms buildup, so that negotiations can
continue without the pressure of a deadline. The goal of such a
step: So long as the superpowers negotiate, there will be no
further arms buildup.

The crucial point is that someone has to start to stop. Who is
the wiser? People claim that the Soviet Union's permanent arms
buildup is forcing us to go on with our own. We can reply to this
thesis with a question: For how long does the West wish to hand
over its freedom to negotiate to the Soviet Union? Doesn't the
person who starts to stop seize the initiative for negotiation?

The East German writer Hermann Kant has said something
that gives us food for thought: "It makes no sense to keep building and deploying nuclear weapons while arduously counting the
old ones. If we are counting in order to reduce the number, then
we don't have to increase the number while we count."

The West should take the Soviet moratorium proposal seriously. It would not imperil our security. The possibility of arming
in order to disarm has turned out to be wishful thinking. After
more than a year of negotiating about a zero solution in Geneva,
the Soviet press agency Novosti announced this response to the
planned NATO arms buildup: "In case of threat, we have no
choice but to make an atomic response. There is no alternative."
And these words came true.

In December 1982, President Reagan announced plans for

the deployment of 100 MX-type intercontinental missiles in the United States. Dimitri Ustinov, Moscow's minister of defense, retorted that the Soviet Union would set up missiles "of the same class." He thus revised an astonishing commentary by *Pravda*, which had written: "The Soviet Union has no intention of vying with and trying to catch up with every new arms system that the United States creates." No indeed, that much common sense cannot be expected from either superpower at this time. The pressure exerted from below on the arms buildup has to grow stronger. The Geneva talks have once again been mainly propaganda. In December 1982, Ustinov said, "Frankly, we doubt the veracity and seriousness of the United States in regard to achieving results that would be acceptable to both sides in Geneva." A few days earlier, U.S. Secretary of Defense Caspar Weinberger had said the same thing about the Soviet Union.

First Steps: 2. No Arms Exports

"We will not become the weapon makers of the world," said Helmut Schmidt, and Helmut Kohl says the same thing. But the fact is that West Germany is today the world's fifth largest weapons exporter. Bonn should strictly limit itself to selling no weapons outside its alliance. If we followed this policy, our gains would be threefold: political, economic, and ethical.

Political gain: By exporting arms to Third World countries, we are constantly creating new enemies. The enemies of all the nations to whom we send weapons will automatically become our enemies. We ourselves are responsible for making these automatic enemies. This policy is foolish and shortsighted. In the long run, all weapons exported outside the alliance will be damaging to German interests. During the 1960's, the Soviet Union filled Egypt and Somalia with weapons; what good does that do the Russians now? Today, both countries are in the opposite camp. The United States once armed Vietnam and Iran to the teeth. Today, both nations are its enemies.

It's bad enough that the superpowers fight out their conflicts inside—and at the expense of—the countries of the Third World. Will the situation get any better for the Third World if the medium-sized powers like West Germany supply them with weapons?

Economic gain: Arms production today is technological, automated big business. The jobs argument is nonsense, if only for purely economic reasons. The manufacture of weapons requires few workers. Indeed, we prevent the creation of new jobs, because our arms exports to the Third World are cutting off markets there. Often, the enemies of the nations that buy our weapons stop buying anything from us. In the long run, this costs us a lot more jobs than can be created in the short run by arms production. Japan, for example, will not export any weapons—and it does business with the entire world. France (even under President François Mitterrand) is sending more and more arms to Third World countries, but fewer and fewer consumer goods.

Did West Germany's consumer exports suffer because we exported (almost) no weapons during the 1950's and 1960's? Why is it so hard for Schmidt and Strauss as economists to understand the economic disadvantages of selling arms abroad? The cause of this economic myopia is the lack of moral questioning and feeling in politics.

For Christians in politics, the decisive aspect here too must be the ethical one. Political ethics requires asking about the sense, goal, and values of our politics and then acting accordingly. What good does it do, however, if we export no weapons and other countries do? This is a frequent criticism. Pointing out someone else's sin is, once again, no ethical justification for one's own sins. *We* are responsible for our arms exports, and no one else. If a nation sets a good example, then it will be heard sooner if it encourages other nations to follow a similar policy and negotiates to get its policy accepted by others.

When it comes to arms exports, a politician's deeds are usually different from his words. There are only three Latin American countries to which West Germany does not export weapons. A few short months after the Falklands War, Argentina once again received German battleships with English(!) engines. Thirty percent of the arms that Argentina used against our NATO ally, England, during the Falklands War came from West Germany. Most Bonn politicians kowtow to the West German armaments industry. The immoral business of West German arms exports functions only because it is blessed in Bonn by a large coalition of cowards. They applaud the pope when he calls for peace and condemns arms exports; but then they give their blessing to irresponsible business deals. The weapons of the rich have seldom prevented war in the countries of the poor; they have often led to war. Far away from us, people have to die because we still justify arms manufacturing with the jobs argument. This is an argument for murder in the full sense of the word. This is a *mortal* sin of our time. Arms exporters do a bang-up business! They sell weapons so that we may have jobs! I would recommend going one step further: Start a war as soon as possible. A war will create even more jobs, both at the front and in defense plants. Eventually, there won't be too many unemployed people left. . . . Weapons for the Third World—this is politically shortsighted, economically senseless, and ethically untenable.

I have outlined the first two steps that I regard as needful, possible, and even indispensable if we are to get beyond our current politics. I know that one can make serious objections here and that my suggestions are not without their risks. There is no guarantee that the Soviets will stop their arms buildup if we stop ours. However, the courage required to take this risk is more realistic and promising than the daredevil tactic of nuclear intimidation. There is no love and no hope without risks, and there is also no peace without risks. Unless we take the first step, the Communist governments will probably not disarm. Instead, they will demand even greater sacrifices from their populations for the sake of the arms buildup. If we do it, then they will certainly do it.

The Soviet Union is not faced with the question of how it can conquer Western Europe. It still has to hold on to Eastern Europe or at least let go of it without losing face. If we refuse to take a chance and attempt the two steps that I have suggested, we will be running even greater risks. Without courage and imagination, no salvation is possible. If (as Franz Kafka phrased it) war is a product of a dreadful lack of imagination, then peace is the product of dreadful imagination.

In the Nuclear Era, we must conquer war, or else war will conquer us. We can be fascinated by death, and also by life. We have to choose. If we are fascinated by death, then we believe in security by way of the bomb. If we are fascinated by life, then we believe in freedom by way of God. In the countries of the Christian West, a depressive, nihilistic mood dominates the end of the twentieth century. We may know almost everything, but we believe in little and hope even less. The fascination with death prevails everywhere. The question is: Can we still return to life? Every journey, no matter how long, begins with the first step in the right direction. The first step toward disarming is a step toward life and away from death. The path of the Sermon on the Mount is *the* road to life.

The Pan-German Peace Movement

For the first time since the division of Germany after 1945, there is something like a truly pan-German idea in Germany. The peace movement has attracted hundreds of thousands of East *and* West Germans and is having an impact on the politics of both countries. Strangely enough, the pan-German peace movement uses no rhetoric about uniting Germany. The idea of peace brings people together. This is important, because the joint effort is an ethical one.

The contrast between the East and West German systems—a contrast that has always been regarded as crucial—has now become unimportant. The chief enemy is neither "socialism" nor "capitalism." The chief enemies on either side are the weapons of annihilation threatening *all* of us together. "On either side of the wall [there are] opposition movements that are one in their motives and goals," says Rudolf Bahro, who served time in an East German prison because of his pacifist views.

Perhaps the pan-German peace movement will actually create a basis for what has been previously called "reunification." It could be that, as Bahro speculates, the key to solving the German question is not so much a reunification in the traditional sense as the demilitarization of both German states. A largely demilitarized Germany without nuclear weapons would hold little terror even for the allies of either German state.

In this century, Germany has begun two world wars. Why shouldn't Germany now *prevent* World War III? We already have a basis for this, since more and more East and West Germans are coming to realize that atomic weapons are a danger and not a shield. Many Germans no longer feel protected by nuclear arms. Politicians now have increasingly to defend these weapons against their constituents. In 1982, 300,000 people attended peace demonstrations in Bonn, 500,000 in Rome, and 700,000 in New York. East Germany has hundreds of peace groups, as do Poland and the Soviet Union. The peace movement is proof that for decades we have repressed our anxieties about nuclear arms. But now, millions of people no longer fear their fear. They are losing their fear of resisting nuclear arms and are becoming capable of resisting them. The prerequisite for this was their realization of their fear of atomic weapons and their acceptance of this fear. If your learn to distinguish between right fear and wrong fear, between founded and unfounded fear, you can become free and resistant. The most important question that the peace movement confronts us with is: How can we escape the nuclear trap? Both peace movements in Germany live on and learn from one another. Each is a prerequisite for and help to the other. Each legitimizes the other, especially in the eyes of the population and the politicians.

The pan-German peace movement poses most sharply the question of the national identity of the Germans. At the Catholic Convention in Düsseldorf, Georg Leber of the Social Democratic Party of West Germany and Alois Mertes of the Christian Democratic Union said they had no objection to a peace movement in West Germany so long as there was one in East Germany too. And the East German peace movement does exist—under the aegis of the church. At internal training functions of East Germany's Socialist Unity Party, the participants are told: What the intellectuals were in Czechoslovakia in 1968 and the workers in Poland in 1980, East German youth can be tomorrow in the East German peace movement. East Germany's Evangelical Church has moved closer to the pacifist positions of the Sermon on the Mount than has West Germany's Evangelical Church. Still, we may hope that the East German church will act as leaven for the West German church, just as the American Catholic Church has done for the Catholic Church in West Germany.

It is no coincidence that the West German peace movement received its defining impulses from the church convention of 1981 in Hamburg. According to Rudolf Bahro, "The resistance of the [anti-Nazi] professing church against the Nazi regime is bearing interest. [Dietrich] Bonhoeffer [a Protestant clergyman and resistance fighter who was executed by the Nazis] is the lodestar of this resurrection"—both in East and in West Germany. (At the end of 1942, Bonhoeffer concealed a note among some roof tiles to keep it from the Gestapo: "Perhaps doomsday will dawn tomorrow; if so, we will be glad to give up our work for a better future. But not before then.")

The peace movement shows that we are not impotent. There are still possibilities for fighting the brutalization and militarization of our lives. The neutron bomb has the capacity "only" to kill people but not to damage property. Now we have a weapon that does the exact opposite: the peace movement. It lets people live and destroys only the instruments of war. The peace movement has left its mark on official politics. Today, Helmut Schmidt and Helmut Kohl are not the only politicians who talk differently about the peace movement. At the first large peace demonstration in Bonn, Helmut Schmidt was still talking about "dubious elements," and Helmut Kohl said he was reminded of Nazi Germany's Popular Front in World War II. In 1980, Henry Kissinger was still saying, "We have to arm in order to disarm." By 1982, he was saying, "The arguments of the strategists are getting more and more irrational; the arguments of the peace movement more and more rational." And Lord Soper, the ex-chairman of the British Methodists: "In the past, the pacifist seemed to be a crazy idealist in the real world; today, he is the realist in a crazy world."

The peace movement can become a liberation movement. However, we have to be liberated not from suffering, but from our inability to suffer; not from grief, but from our inability to grieve; not from powerlessness, but from too much power; not from poverty, but from our wealth; not from insecurity, but from our security complex; and not from our realism, but from our blindness to realities. However, only those who liberate themselves can be liberated.

Today's peace movements in the East and West finally offer us a chance to turn the peace *for* nations, for which the politicians were responsible, into a peace *of* nations, for which we are all responsible.

The Politics of the Sermon on the Mount

The politics of the Sermon on the Mount is a politics of peace. A politics of peace is more than a politics of security. Peace is more than not killing. Peace is action. Peace and development here and in the Third World are inseparable. Peace and exploitation of nature are incompatible. It could be that, even without atomic weapons, we will end any life worth living on this blue planet.

Jesus describes peace as gentle and humble. Meekness, goodness, and humility are more than passive nonviolence. Peace does not mean securing jobs by exporting weapons. Arms exports kill. World War III began long ago for many people in the Third World.

Peace demands an overall reversal and repentance. Peace begins when we understand that we have to live in a different way, so that others can live at all. Not only do our weapons kill, but our lifestyle kills.

Saint Paul said that we cannot have peace with God if we do not create peace among men. Peace is more than the absence of war. The peace of the Sermon on the Mount is the opposite of violence, not just the opposite of war. This peace is also more than détente. Détente (as proved by the fearful reactions of some left-wing détente politicians to the suppression of Solidarity in Poland) can also be a graveyard politics. There are wars in the midst of peace. "The big battlefield is everyday life in society," said the Italian critic of psychiatry, Franco Basaglia.

There is no peace so long as work is structured in such a way that every tenth person in the industrial nations and every second person in the developing countries is unemployed. There is no peace so long as for men—and increasingly for women—career is more important than home, spouse, family, and children. Many children grow up semiorphaned, without a father—not a condition that makes us optimistic about a more peaceful world. There is no peace so long as our society is based unilaterally on male principles and not integrally on human principles. There is no peace so long as economics remains the world of men and love the world of women. There is no peace so long as masculinity is confused with "strength" and femininity with "weakness." There is no peace so long as 100,000 babies a year are killed in their mother's womb in a rich country like West Germany—mostly for "economic" reasons. There is no peace so long as we put up with the 13,000 yearly traffic deaths that our motorized way of life demands. There is no peace so long as people torture animals and wipe out whole species. There is no peace so long as we claim that right makes might and yet think nothing of forcing our might upon the rights of all feeling nonhuman creatures. The Sermon on the Mount suggests that we overcome fear by means of trust and that we create trust in every possible way. It opens up vistas that we ordinary citizens can scarcely believe. In the middle of the Sermon, we find the Lord's Prayer. Jesus prays, attacking the value system of his time. He prays against violence and glory, power and money, security and enmity. If you would like to pray but can't, then speak the words of this prayer slowly, and you will begin to understand the preacher on the mount.

The peace of the Sermon on the Mount is based on values: radical freedom and radical responsibility. Jesus' peace has its price: commitment to the suffering, the hungry, the battered, the outcast. Solidarity in Poland was a peace movement because it was a nonviolent struggle for justice and freedom. The Cape

Anamur Committee, whose rescue ship saved 9,508 Vietnamese refugees from the ocean, was a peace movement. The Helsinki groups in Moscow and Charta 77 in Prague are peace movements. Jesus says that the peacemakers are blessed, not the peace talkers. If you help to feed a child in the Third World, you are a pacifist, a peacemaker in the spirit of Jesus. The pacifism of the Sermon on the Mount is not identical with conscientious objection (to the surprise of many, soldiers get a fair shake from Jesus: the captain of Caparnaum, the captain under the cross, and others). Pax Christi is more. Edward Schillebeeckx explains: "After all, we are striving for the ultimate goal: peace as a work of worldwide justice." Anyone can work toward this goal, not only politicians.

However, in order to prevent the huge and irrevocable catastrophe, we first have to get rid of all atomic missiles. We still won't have peace, but we'll at least have a basis for a fight for peace. Peace may not be everything, but in the Atomic Era everything is nothing without peace. The Sermon on the Mount and nuclear missiles are incompatible. Helmut Gollwitzer defines the first goal of the Sermon today: "The removal of all nuclear weapons from German soil on both sides [of the Wall]—Europe as a nuclear-free zone—a nuclear-free world, and the billions spent on armaments to be used for making the earth livable." As a Christian, I consider the politics of the bomb unacceptable. A world without atomic bombs is still not a sound world, but a world full of atomic bombs will eventually not be a world.

The Christianity of Jesus of Nazareth has helped us to eliminate human sacrifice and slavery. Why shouldn't it help today, along with other religions, to make *the* decisive contribution to a peace ethics as a prerequisite for peace? Where else are the ethical resources of a humane world if not in Buddhism and Hinduism, in Judaism and Christianity, in Islam and Shintoism? The Sermon on the Mount is the spiritual resource of mankind. It is waiting to be discovered. But it can be discovered only by each individual. And the individuals who have to discover it include the politicians. One can't govern with the Sermon on the Mount? Today, one can govern *only* with the Sermon on the Mount. If you get involved with it, you will begin to sense that the end of fear and the start of freedom are waiting here. Helmut Kohl once confirmed my feeling that this private experience also exists in politics. During the 1976 election campaign, the candidate for chancellor said in many speeches, "Everything that is good and right in private life is good and right in politics."

That statement has been haunting me. It was an important stage on my road toward discovering the politics of the Sermon on the Mount. Gandhi, who knew a great deal about the Sermon, said, "Today we are continually being astounded at the discoveries made in the area of violence. I can guarantee that far more astonishing and seemingly impossible discoveries can be made in the area of nonviolence."

If you reject the love of enemies in the Sermon on the Mount as unrealistic, then consider for one moment the real consequences of enmity. In its present-day political structure, the world is the result of some 6,000 years of organized warfare. In our century alone, at least 200 million human beings have been killed by wars—i.e. hatred of enemies. It is our duty to remember this, not to forget it. A third world war will probably claim billions of victims, and no one will be able to remember them. The Sermon on the Mount is the Magna Carta of a total and integral peace for all people in all times. It could even inspire and motivate politicians to follow a politics of peace worthy of the name. In 1965, Pope Paul VI told a plenary session of the U.N., "If you wish to be brothers, then put down your arms. One cannot love with assault weapons in one's hands!"

Many Christians today believe more in the power of the bomb than in the power of the Sermon on the Mount. The politics of the bomb is a God-is-dead politics. The politics of the bomb is the practice of forgetting God. This atheism is revealed not so much in atheistic ideology as in the scorn for life. If you see meaning in life, then, as a responsible politician, you cannot evoke biological nihilism.

The Sermon on the Mount is a protest against nihilism.

The Sermon on the Mount sets hope against despair.

The Sermon on the Mount sees love as stronger than hate.

The Sermon on the Mount is a remedy for our emotional retardation.

Gandhi was once asked by Christian missionaries what they would have to do to get the Hindus to accept the Sermon. His reply: "Think of the secret of the rose. Everyone likes a rose because it is fragrant. Be fragrant, gentlemen!"

Christians must have the scent of the Sermon on the Mount.

The Sermon on the Mount or the End of History

The Eastern threat is as real for the West as the Western threat for the East. In this situation, the danger of an irrational action is as great in Moscow as in Washington. The West German newspaper *Frankfurter Allgemeine* once published an editorial defending the arms escalation with the argument that "in a certain sense, it [was] a desperate act."

Seldom has there been such an exact definition of what the arms buildup means. Acts of desperation are always irrational. You let yourself be forced to do something that you really don't want to do. And just why do we let ourselves be forced? Can we seriously hope to escape the vicious circle of the arms race in this way? Don't we then have to fear the next "desperate act" by the Soviets? Won't each "desperate act" keep leading to the next, until the world blows up? Hasn't that always been the case throughout history? Are the Soviet SS-20's rendered harmless by

American cruise missiles and Pershings? After a nuclear war, no life will remain—at least in Europe. Since none of us wants this, we should not allow ourselves to be forced into the "desperate act" of escalation. No one can force us except ourselves. In 1975, *Bild*, a West German newspaper, polemized against launching ramps for nuclear missiles on West German soil: "No power in the world, not even NATO, can force us to accept them against our will." I admire the farsightedness of my colleagues. At the time, I hadn't gotten that far.

Sensible politics does not try to make a dangerous situation even more dangerous through a nuclear arms buildup. The only rational decision today is to try to dismantle the danger very cautiously. Any country that keeps escalating its arms has not yet grasped *the* lesson of history: An explosion has always come when there were too many guns. But why are we too arrogant to learn from history even in the Atomic Era? The hope that we can develop offensive weapons without ever using them is a dangerous daydream.

The breather we have been enjoying in Europe since 1945 is still no world peace. While the cannon have remained silent here, 130 wars have been fought, primarily in the Third World. The result: 50 million dead—as many as in World War II. Governments will change their policies only if their citizens change. Citizens have to change their governments. The arms buildup is a mental illness. If we keep spending a lot more money on armaments than on fighting starvation, we will be preparing our spiritual and then our physical death. We still have Gethsemane 2,000 years later: Jesus denied and in danger of being nailed to the cross—and his followers asleep. Yes, indeed: We ourselves keep crucifying him—in every starving child, with our every act of violence, even private violence, and with the billions we spend on armaments.

Even worse than our ethical immaturity concerning the Sermon on the Mount are our good consciences. Christianity is in danger of becoming what Hanna Wolff calls a "magic-cow religion." You can milk it at any time and use it toward any end, even so-called just wars.

The permanent lulling of human responsibility, our constantly passing the buck to God may be the true failure of Christians today. Jesus wants us as "fellow workers," not as "slaves of God." Jesus rejects the image of man as a slave just as he rejects a patriarchal image of God.

Jesus calls those blessed who are nonviolent, who make peace, who love their enemies. These things aren't supposed to happen at some point in the future; they have to happen here and now. The God that church practice has projected beyond the clouds has been heightened to utter meaninglessness. God the Father, whom Jesus talks about, is a God of love. Jesus is quite clear: "Seek, and you will find; . . . Every one then who hears these words of mine and does them will be like a wise man who built his house upon the rock." And anyone who does not follow Jesus' words is a moron.

One cannot govern with the Sermon on the Mount? Without it, there will soon be neither governments nor governed. The radical changes in science and in weapons technology have to be followed by an equally radical change in our political institutions and, above all, in our consciousness. The crossroads at which we are standing today was described by Jesus in the Peace Gospel of the Essenes:* "No man can serve two masters. He serves either death or life."

Without the Sermon on the Mount, we will approach the

---

*Edmont B. Székely discovered the Aramaic writings of the Essene sects in the secret archives of the Vatican during the 1920's. He translated them, and his word was confirmed by the Qumran finds on the Dead Sea in 1947. A great deal of the spirit of the Sermon on the Mount becomes understandable when we read the Peace Gospel of the Essenes. Five million Americans have read it since 1934. Arnold Toynbee called the Essenes the "only practical mystics in history."

end of history. Saint Augustine said, "We should love our enemies, not because they are already our brothers, but so that they may become our brothers." A new era began with Jesus. Now, 2,000 years later, it is our job to begin a new era, an era without war. The journey of the Sermon is no pleasure stroll, but it is nevertheless a journey to freedom. Jesus said, "My burden is light." The God of Jesus wants to liberate, not burden us.

Peace Is Possible

Is peace possible? Human beings have always wanted peace, and politicians and military men have always waged war. When has history ever known a peace worthy of the name?

Aren't human beings violent and unpeaceful by nature? Is peace truly possible, given these biological considerations? Is man not a wolf to man? No doubt, a lot of big, bad wolves are running around in our society and in world politics. Thomas Hobbes said that man is a wolf to man, but we have always projected this image onto other people: onto society, onto enemies. Meanwhile, however, a lot of people are beginning to realize that the real wolf is inside *ourselves.*

We can recognize and control the wolf only by means of self-knowledge in the sense of the inscription KNOW THYSELF at Apollo's temple in Delphi. Apollo was the god of moderation, order, and clarity. However, Apollo had a surrogate and counterpart, Dionysus. Dionysus embodied disorder, the netherworld, chaos. Self-knowledge is, first of all, the painful realization that we are constantly torn between Apollo and Dionysus, between good and evil. In each of us there is a Dionysus, a wolf, a portion of evil.

Self-knowledge, however, is the knowledge of good in us, the knowledge of the divine core in our souls. It means remembering that we are the image of God, that we come from God and return to God. It is the struggle against making the image of man as well as man himself materialistic. We are not the lords of nature; we are the children of nature.

The psychoanalyst Horst Eberhard Richter said, "Each of us certainly has an aggressive drive component. But it is equally indisputable that man, in contrast to animals, can siphon his aggressive impulses into socially harmless channels. No historian in the world has ever found a direct causal link between aggressive instincts and the instigation of wars." Erich Fromm found it "absurd" to imagine that human beings are by nature doomed to war.

For the past 170 years, neither Sweden nor Switzerland has fought a single war. I do not have the impression that there is anything wrong with the Swedes or the Swiss.

Anyone who sees war as "inevitable" has been labeled "insane" by the pope and the secretary-general of the United Nations. I consider it remarkable that Valentin Falin, the former Soviet ambassador to West Germany, declared in 1982 that, if we regard war as our fate, then we are creating a "psychological infrastructure" for wars.

Western European politics since 1945 shows that peace is possible. My mother and father had it pounded into their heads that France is Germany's hereditary enemy. Today, experience has taught us how ridiculous that was. In the Middle Ages, towns without walls were a utopian idea. One hundred thirty years ago, many people who read *Uncle Tom's Cabin* considered Harriet Beecher Stowe's plea for the abolition of slavery utopian. Political superstition can occasionally be overcome. All it takes is the realization by at least a minority that, if the world is in trouble, they themselves are in trouble. Inner reversal—repentance—is certainly the most difficult reversal, but it is not impossible. Repent, says Jesus. Become active, change your fear into trust.

Today, when we consider a duel an anachronistic way of

settling private differences, why shouldn't more and more people regard the preparation for nuclear holocaust as anachronistic? The atomic war does not have to come. Peace can and must exist, especially in the Atomic Era.

There will always be homicidal and suicidal maniacs, but they don't have to gain political control. In 1972, the United States and China thought they had to protect themselves against one another militarily. Today, we no longer have to fear a war between the capitalist superpower and the Communist giant. Why should a similar development between the Soviet Union and the United States and between Eastern and Western Europe be impossible? If defense is possible only at the price of annihilation, then the only rational response to this "defense" is no. It is not the arms buildup that is rational, but only a no to the arms buildup.

Albert Einstein felt that mankind could not survive without a fundamental rethinking. A new security policy demands new thinking. Annihilatory weapons are not the cause but the consequence of annihilatory thinking. Such thinking has to be replaced by thinking about security and confidence. Security is the ability to defend oneself, not the ability to wipe out the other side. Legitimate security thinking has given way to a security complex, pathological security thinking.

The pathology of our official thinking on security was demonstrated by Helmut Schmidt when he glorified the MRCA Tornado program as the "greatest arms system since the birth of Christ." We have reached the top of the nuclear mountain and are now standing on the brink of disaster. We have to climb down rather than continue the brinkmanship of the arms race. Our brinkmanship, the way we whistle a happy tune and say, "It'll all work out"—these are signs of feeblemindedness. Now is the time to take the Sermon on the Mount to heart. We have to turn around before we plunge over the edge. Stopping and turning back are no guarantees that the other side will stop and turn back; but they are the best prerequisites.

In the Peace Gospel of the Essenes, Jesus, who was probably an Essene himself, tells a small group of disciples about peace: "Seek the angel of peace in everything that lives, in everything you do, in every word you speak. For peace is the key to all knowledge, to every secret, to all life." Those who hear his words and live accordingly are, says Jesus, "children of light."

For all the open or subliminal theories of violence that theologians and princes of the church still occasionally read into Jesus' teachings, we must firmly remember—without ifs, ands, or buts—that Jesus rejects violence, he is *the* man of peace. His teachings are unequivocal; they are joyous and not ominous tidings. Bring peace by first becoming peaceful yourselves. Bring peace by dismantling your images of the enemy. The Sermon on the Mount does not make extraordinary demands that place it beyond politics. However, it does make extraordinary demands upon politicians. The Sermon thinks politics from beginning to end, and to the ultimate end. It demands that we always think of the consequences of political acts, the consequences of arms escalation. It shows Christians their responsibility for their deeds. The Sermon on the Mount confronts us with a choice: God or the bomb? You cannot serve two masters: God *and* the bomb, peace *and* preparations for war.

Jesus offers children as an example for adults. Children may fight, but they never kill one another.

The Sermon on the Mount has always been understood from some point of view: exegetic, scholarly, historical, eschatological, messianic, utopian, theological. But it has never been truly understood—as a whole. We have to read it exactly as it is written, and we have to live accordingly. The Sermon can make the tree of peace blossom—so long as we tend it.

The Sermon on the Mount is a collection of essential utter-

ances by Jesus. These utterances are reliable. Jesus was no oppor-
tunist. He never exaggerated. Anyone who deals with Jesus can
experience this personally. And if you experience it personally,
you don't have to believe; you *know.* You know that Jesus' teachings are a bridge between man and God. Today, the gap between
man and God is gigantic. Thus, bridges are all the more necessary.
The bridge to a life in the Creator's sense is precisely the Sermon
on the Mount. Politicians too can use this bridge if they wish to.
How do politicians know that one can't govern with the Sermon if
they don't try? Heinrich Albertz told Helmut Schmidt, "I get the
impression more and more that the basic rules of Jesus' life and
teachings are the only chance [Germany] has to survive as a
nation."

We will have understood the Sermon on the Mount once we
begin to live as if peace depended solely on us ourselves. Everything else is an evasion of our responsibility and leads to passiv-
ity, resignation, and fatalism.

Dietrich Bonhoeffer said, "Only the man who screams for the
Jews has the right to sing a Gregorian chant." Today, this means:
Only those who fight for peace have the right to pray. A Chris-
tian cannot separate political deeds from religious deeds.

The Sermon on the Mount does not try to comfort us by
saying, Things'll work out somehow. It comforts us by saying,
Things can work out if we make them work out. On the cross-
beam of a crucifix at a charitable organization, I saw an inscription in place of the crucified hands: I HAVE NO HANDS BUT
YOURS. These words struck me like a sudden illumination: everything depends on *us.* Throughout history, war has always been a
reality. The new reality is that in Europe in the age of "mutually
assured destruction" there can be no wars with any chance of
survival. It is a historical truth that war has always been a means
of politics. The new truth is that war can never again be a means
of politics. In the old politics, there may have been "just wars."

In the new politics, there are neither just nor unjust wars, but only annihilation unless so-called national sovereignty is turned into a relative value.

Nuclear war is against creation and thus against the Creator. The new politics means disarmament. The new religion means taking the Sermon on the Mount seriously at last.

Our knowledge, our banal philosophies of progress, which let us do anything we can do, prevent us from being human even more than do the externals of present-day life. Our dependence on science is even more dangerous than our dependence on economics. Our goal is to *be*, not to *know*. The Sermon on the Mount not only cancels out the meaning of having, but it also cancels out the meaning of our knowledge, by invoking the meaning of love. Knowledge without conscience is the ruin of our souls, just as freedom without responsibility is the ruin of freedom. The freedom of the Sermon on the Mount is responsible freedom.

Arthur Miller, the playwright, once flew from New York to California. Next to him sat the chief engineer of a big petroleum company. As they soared across the huge Nevada desert, Miller said to his neighbor, "Well, that's one thing human beings won't be able to change."

"Oh, sure," said the chief engineer. "We can settle at least thirty million people in the desert down there."

"But there's no water," Miller protested.

Oh, but there was, explained the engineer. A gigantic ocean lay underneath the desert. The water could be brought to the surface with three precise atomic explosions.

"But wouldn't the water be radioactive?" Miller asked.

The engineer replied, "That's not my department."

We do not know too little; we now know too much. What we lack is not information, but orientation.

The Sermon on the Mount does not attack reason, it attacks

things that many people call reasonable and normal. It is no surrogate for thinking or for the scholarly study of peace. If we want to find a way out of our ecological crisis, we need more, not less rationality; we need responsible rationality, a rationality that knows its limits. The Sermon on the Mount is a school for human rationality. I am convinced that human beings can learn. I believe in the buried and undiscovered reserves of love and intelligence within us. Anyone who wants to, can open them up.

At the threshold to the third millennium after Christ, we have no other choice. Whether we are socialists or capitalists is random. But we cannot make our survival a random matter. Just as today's global dangers have come from us, from our age-old actions, so too we can conquer the dangers within us by means of new actions.

On June 11, 1982, a rabbi prayed in front of 10,000 people during the U.N. conference on disarmament:

> You did not destroy Hiroshima—
> we did it.
> You did not send the children to the concentration camps—
> we did it.
> You did not pollute our world—
> we did it.
> But today we declare
> that we choose life
> so that our children may live.

Politics without a nuclear threat would not be heaven on earth, but we would probably escape hell on earth. Our goal must be: "Create peace without weapons." The realistic path to this goal: "Create peace with fewer and fewer weapons." Many people find this path and this goal unrealistic. But what is their alternative? If there has been no peace so far, this does not mean that there can be no peace in the Atomic Age. Something that was impossible yesterday *can* be possible today. Albert Schweitzer, who received the Nobel Prize for peace in 1954, said, "Certain truths have remained ineffectual for a long time only because the possibility that they could become realities was not taken into consideration."

For many people today, peace is still a heresy. But let me remind you that almost every new truth came in the guise of a heresy and was fought. Something that seems difficult is not impossible. On January 1, 1983, the Catholic bishops of East Germany asked in a pastoral letter, "Doesn't the often derided ideal of nonviolence, as proclaimed by Jesus in the Sermon on the Mount, gain a rational expressive force that was previously unsuspected?" Rationality and ethics are no longer contradictory—when will West German bishops make this statement? Or are the West German bishops less courageous in regard to the Christian Democratic Union and the Christian Socialist Union than the East German bishops in regard to the Socialist Unity Party? Anyone who called for an end to child labor 100 years ago, anyone who wanted to stop slavery 300 years ago, anyone who said that the earth revolved around the sun 500 years ago, anyone who said that the plague could be conquered 800 years ago—was laughed at. We have to prevent our modern-day plague, nuclear war, by getting rid of the nuclear bombs. We have no other choice. "You have heard that it was said to the men of old . . . But I say to you." This is the new reality and the new authority. "He taught them as one having authority." At the end of the Sermon on the Mount, Matthew writes that "the crowds were astonished at his teaching." We can imagine the "realists" back then shaking their heads at so much "nonsense" and "naiveté." And once again let me ask the question that we must repeatedly ask the "realistic politicians" today: What is your alternative to the armaments madness and the politics of annihilation, if not Jesus' idea that we love our enemies?

Not everyone has to be a pacifist. We would be a lot closer to peace if everyone *wanted* to be a pacifist. The Sermon on the Mount is not an actual reality, but a possible reality. We should act accordingly because we *can* act accordingly. The Sermon is *the* concrete utopia. Everything depends on our willpower. Jesus' elementary question to those he healed was: Do you *want* to be healthy? Many said yes, but with reservations. Peace with reservations: that is the prerequisite for peace. If peace has been "only" a dream so far, then it is high time in the Atomic Era that we disobeyed the prohibition against dreaming. Peace is no problem that we can solve once and for all. It is a reality toward which we must work. And in politics, only the person who works on himself can work toward peace. There is no neutrality in the issue of peace. The peace of the Sermon on the Mount is no noncommittal wish for peace, it is a hard-line practice of peace. Peace is like love. It flees from any relationship if at least one person does not do something for it. There is no love without working toward love; there is no peace without working toward peace. In the Peace Gospel of the Essenes, Jesus says, "Happy are they who *struggle* for peace." We can create peace by striving toward self-knowledge and then self-realization. Self-realization is not egoism. It is what frees us so that we can achieve true solidarity. It is ultimately religious striving. Religious striving is striving for a truly humane life, which, as Helmut Barz puts it, "tries to overcome man's self-involvement as well as the supposedly absolute beyondness of God, so that self-realization can be man's finite answer to God's becoming human."

This book is not a theological study of the Sermon on the Mount. I wanted to present my personal experience with the Sermon. And that was the basis for my ideas and suggestions for a politics of the Sermon on the Mount.

The new, 2,000-year-old image of man in the Sermon on the

Mount is a call: Decide against the law of violence and retaliation and in favor of the law of love and forgiveness. Remember
that you are human beings, and forget everything else. Work
toward overcoming the most inhuman of all dogmas, which
claims that man is incorrigible. The churches have always taught
us that the world is without salvation and that salvation comes
without the world. However, we have known since the Sermon
on the Mount that salvation does not exist without the world
and that the world does not exist without salvation. If we all
work together toward healing and saving the world, then we will
understand and experience the same thing: Peace is possible.